D1036899

Adrienne Barman

CREATUREPEDIA

WELCOME TO THE GREATEST SHOW ON EARTH

WIDE EYED EDITIONS

Contents

CREATUREPEDIA celebrates the amazing array of animals that grace our planet. Sadly, some are now under threat, some are already extinct (and one or two may never have existed in the first place!), but each one has its own unique part to play in the animal kingdom...

Turn the page to see the greatest show on Earth and discover who is the biggest, the brainiest, and the most beautiful of them all.

The architects
Social weaver
builds the largest nest of any bird

The architects

Beaver
builds a dam from logs, mud,
and stones to keep predators away
Weaver ant
works with others to
weave leaves together
to make a nest

Prairie dog burrow has sleeping chambers, nursery chambers, and chambers for hiding from hunters

Taveta weaver
male weaver builds nest, female chooses mate based on quality of nest
Spider
spins a strong web
Mason wasp
female builds a tiny mud nest, stocked with food, for each of her eggs

Sand martin
burrows a nest in a sandy cliff face
Red ovenbird
builds a mud nest that looks like a wood-fired oven
Termite
works with others to build enormous mounds

The big-eared beasts

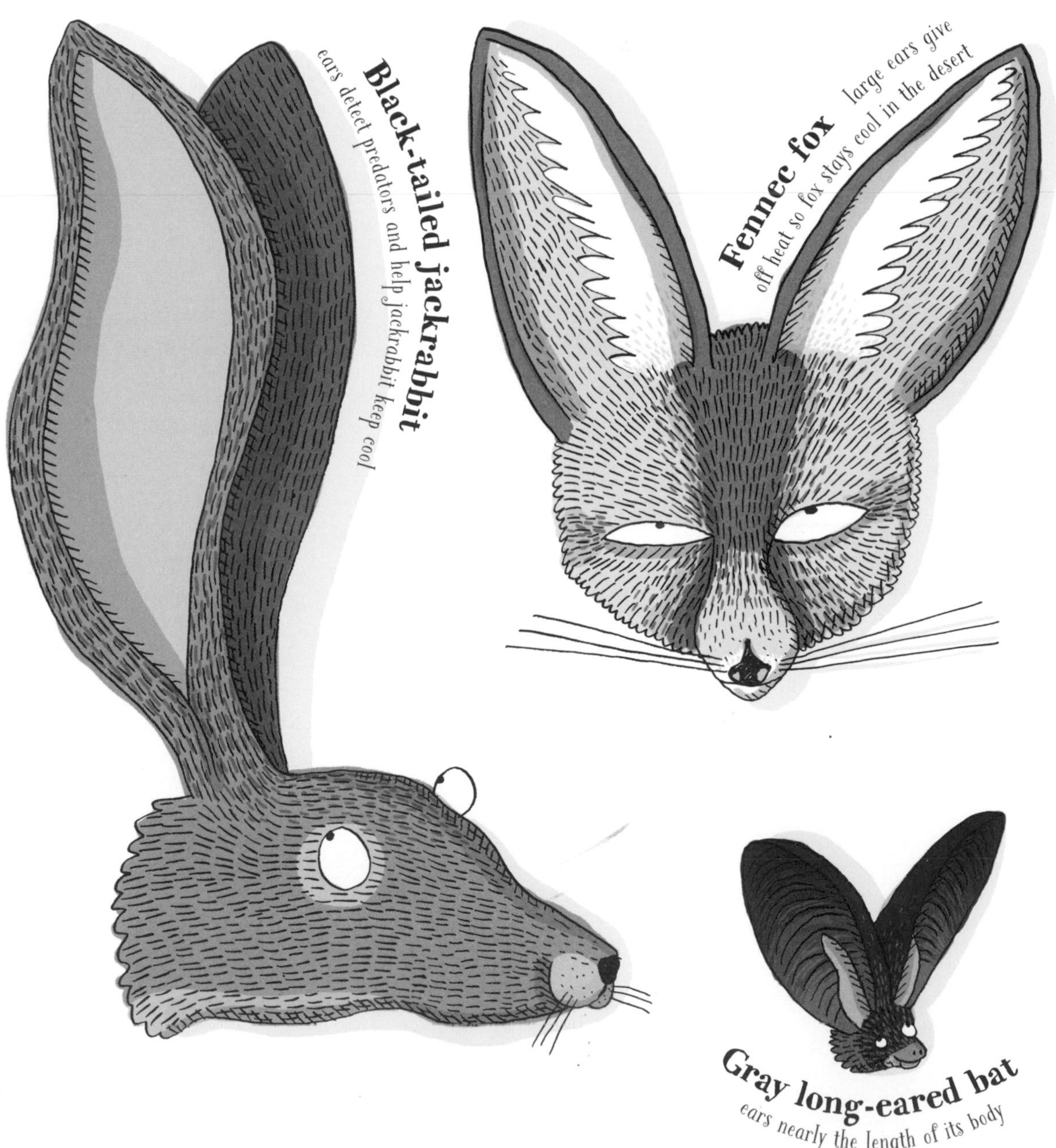

Black-tailed jackrabbit
ears detect predators and help jackrabbit keep cool
Fennec fox
large ears give off heat so fox stays cool in the desert
Gray long-eared bat
ears nearly the length of its body

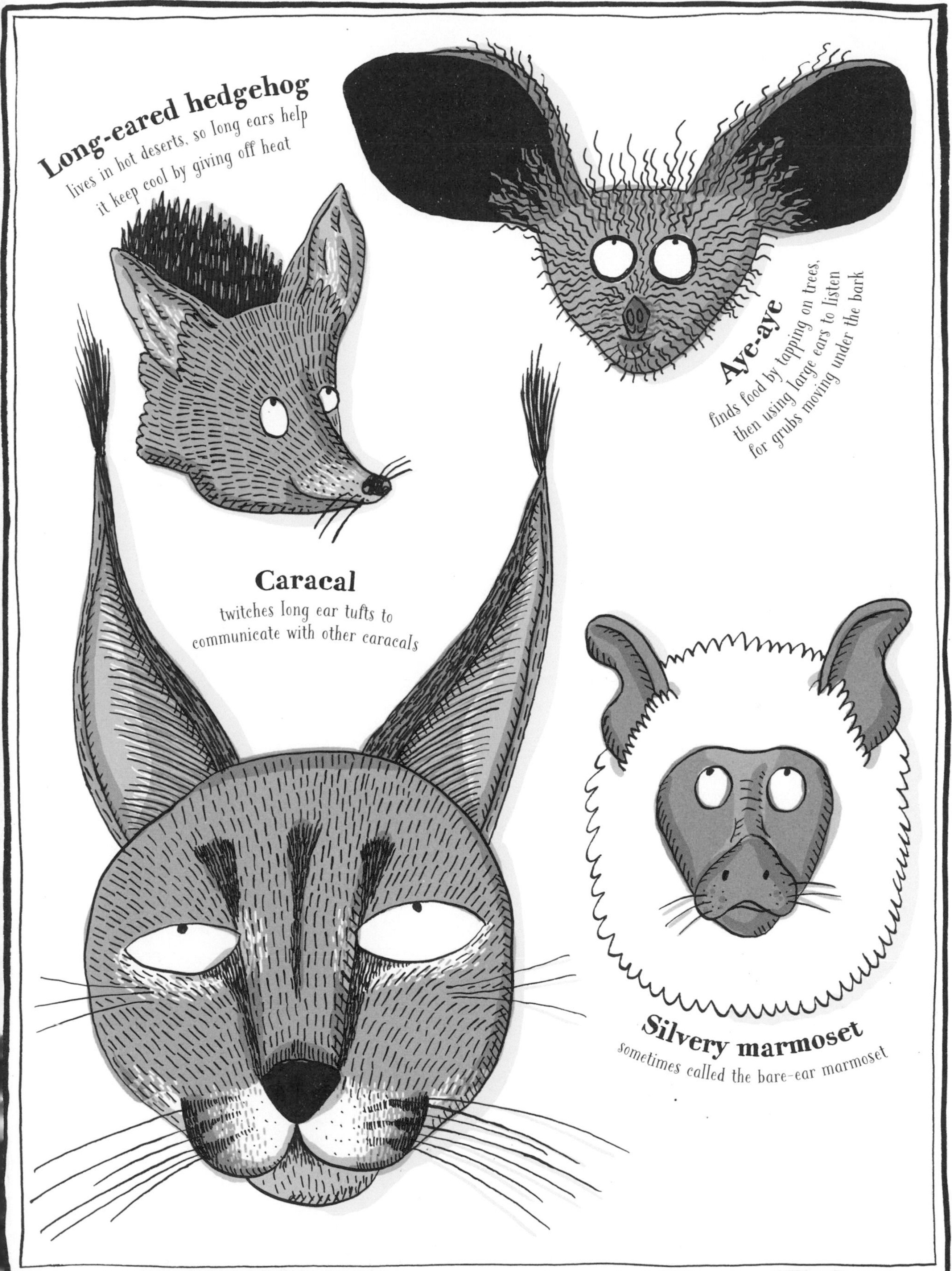
Long-eared hedgehog
lives in hot deserts, so long ears help
it keep cool by giving off heat
Aye-aye
finds food by tapping on trees,
then using large ears to listen
for grubs moving under the bark
Caracal
twitches long ear tufts to
communicate with other caracals
Silvery marmoset
sometimes called the bare-ear marmoset

The big-eared beasts

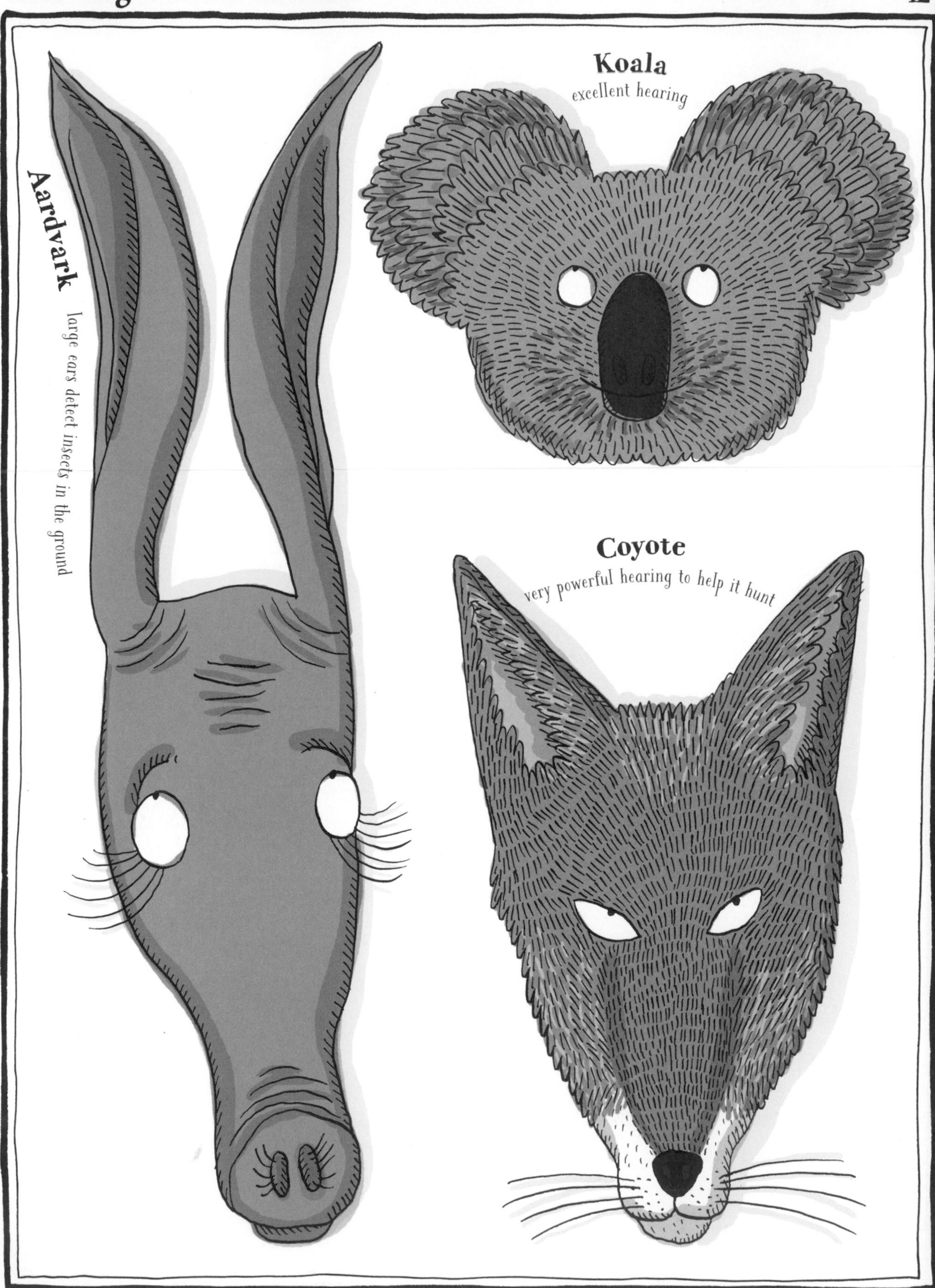
Aardvark
large ears detect insects in the ground
Koala
excellent hearing
Coyote
very powerful hearing to help it hunt

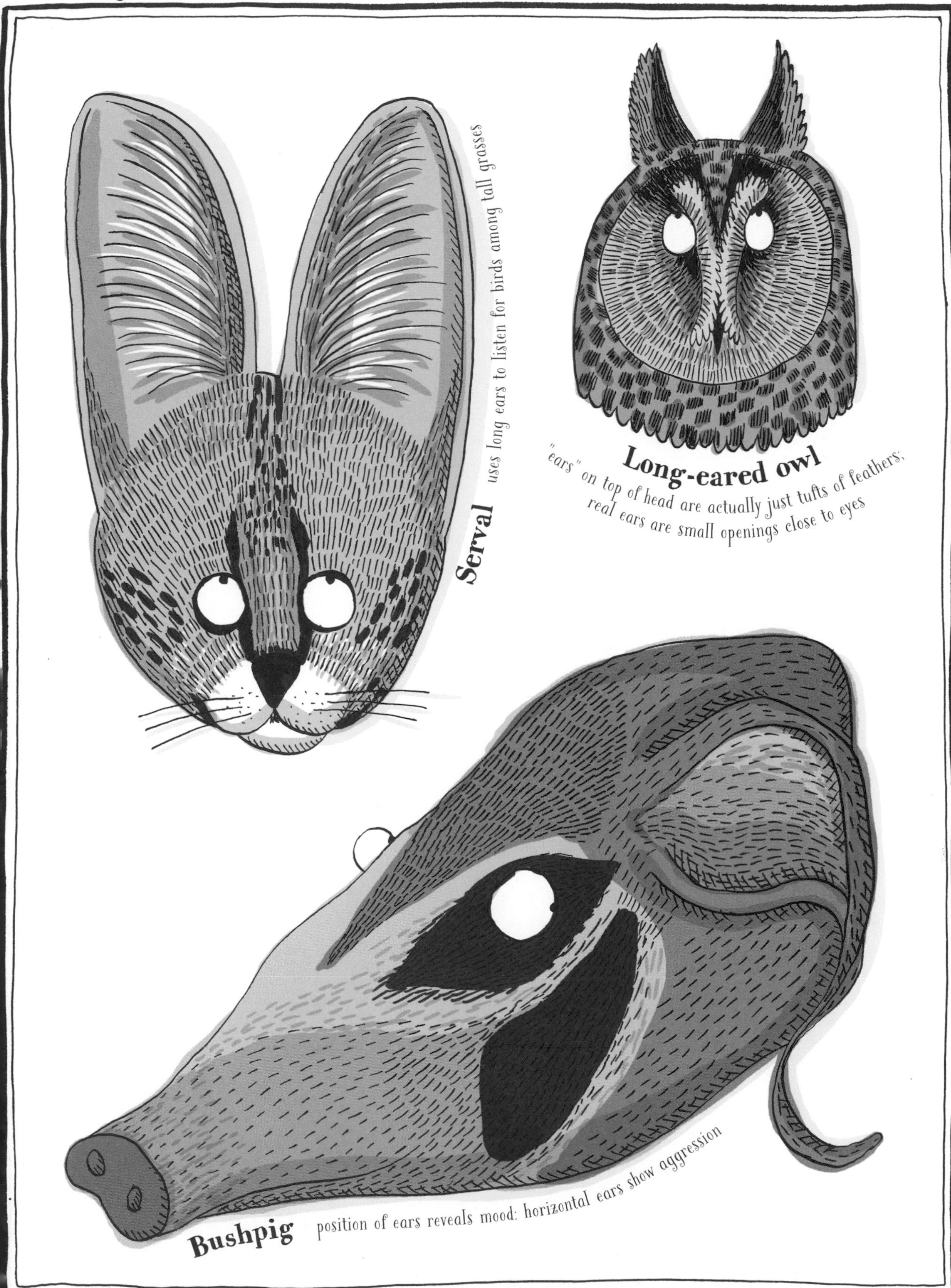
Serval
uses long ears to listen for birds among tall grasses
Long-eared owl
"ears" on top of head are actually just tufts of feathers;
real ears are small openings close to eyes
Bushpig
position of ears reveals mood: horizontal ears show aggression

The big mouths

Northern gannet

Helmeted guinea fowl
Natterjack toad
male call can be heard several miles away
Field cricket
makes sounds by rubbing its wings together

Robin
Blue jay
Jay
Song thrush

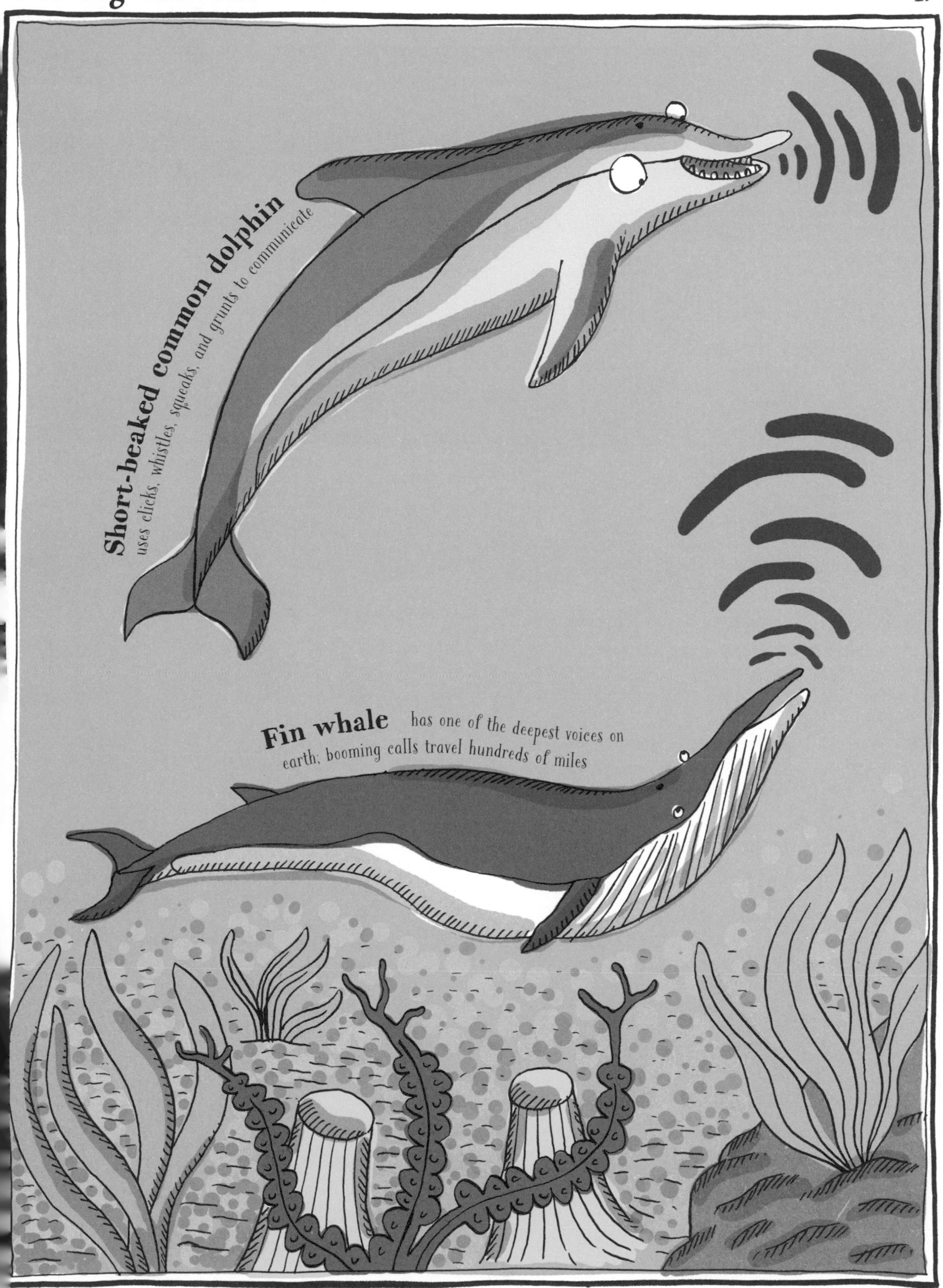
Short-beaked common dolphin
uses clicks, whistles, squeaks, and grunts to communicate
Fin whale has one of the deepest voices on earth; booming calls travel hundreds of miles

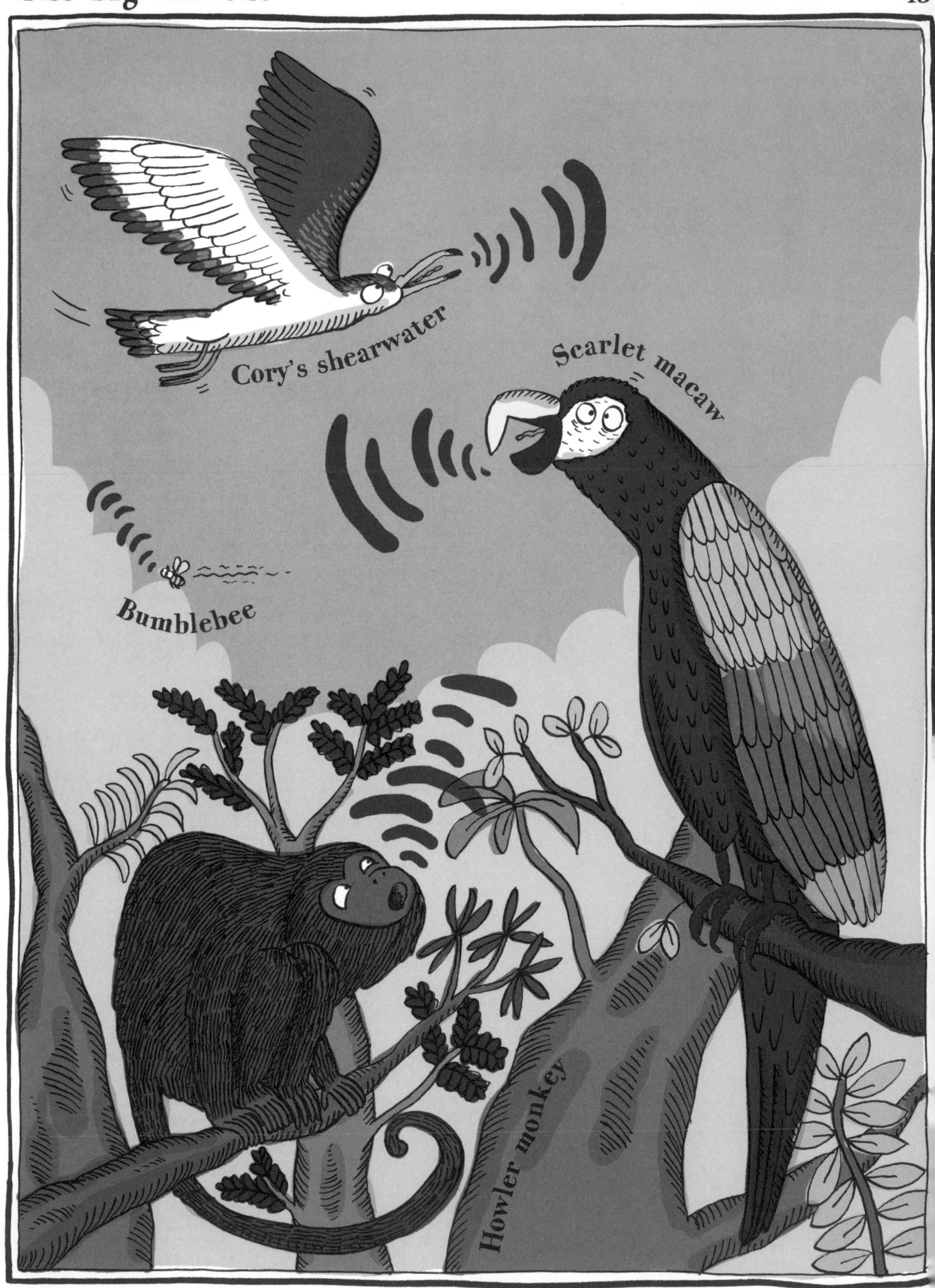
Cory's shearwater
Scarlet macaw
Bumblebee
Howler monkey

Cicada
one of the noisiest insects in the world;
can make a sound over 100 decibels!
Rattlesnake
has hollow segments on the end of its tail
that knock together to make rattling sound
White-fronted goose

The blue beauties

Victoria crowned pigeon

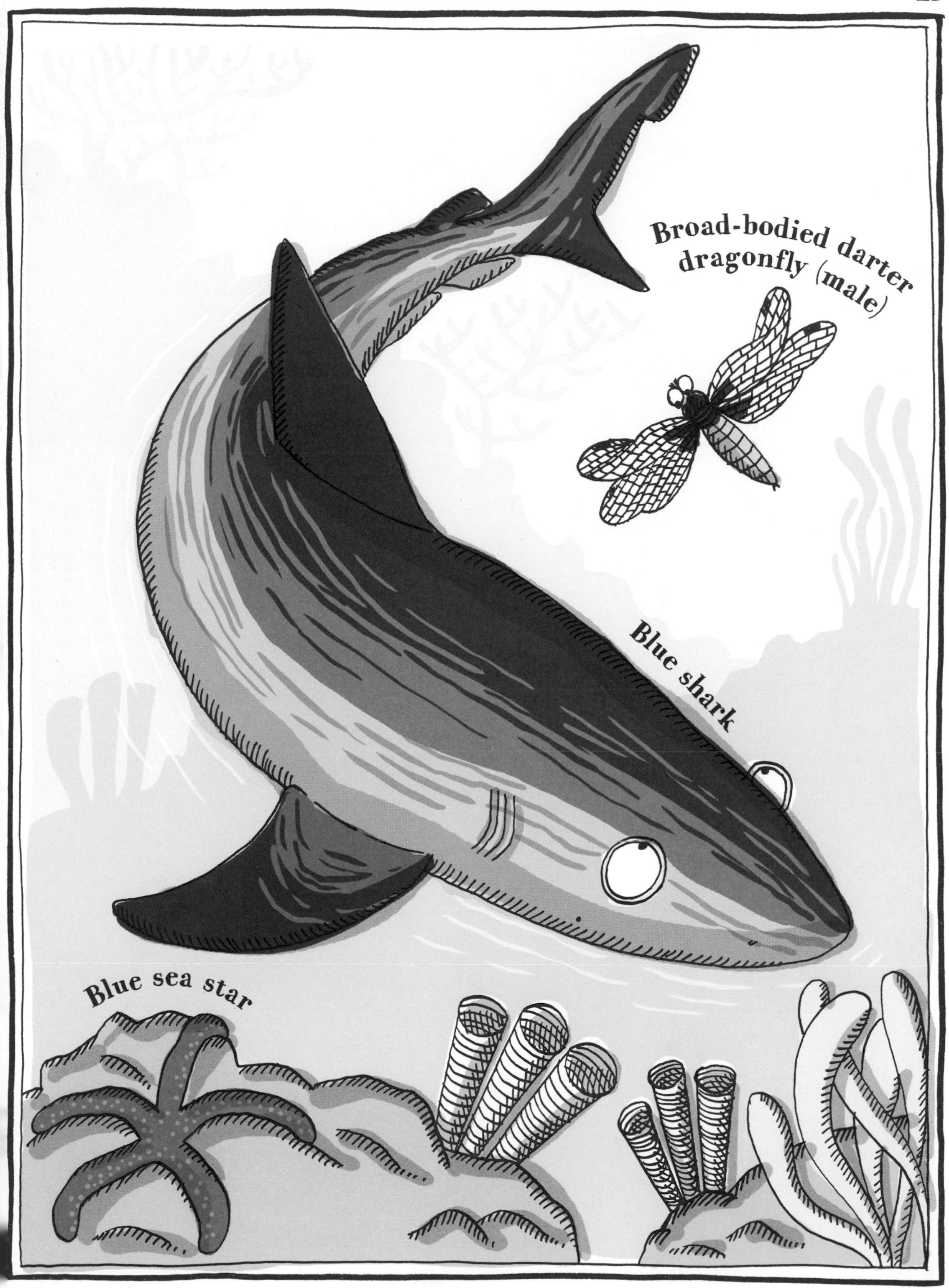
Broad-bodied darter dragonfly (male)
Blue shark
Blue sea star

The blue beauties

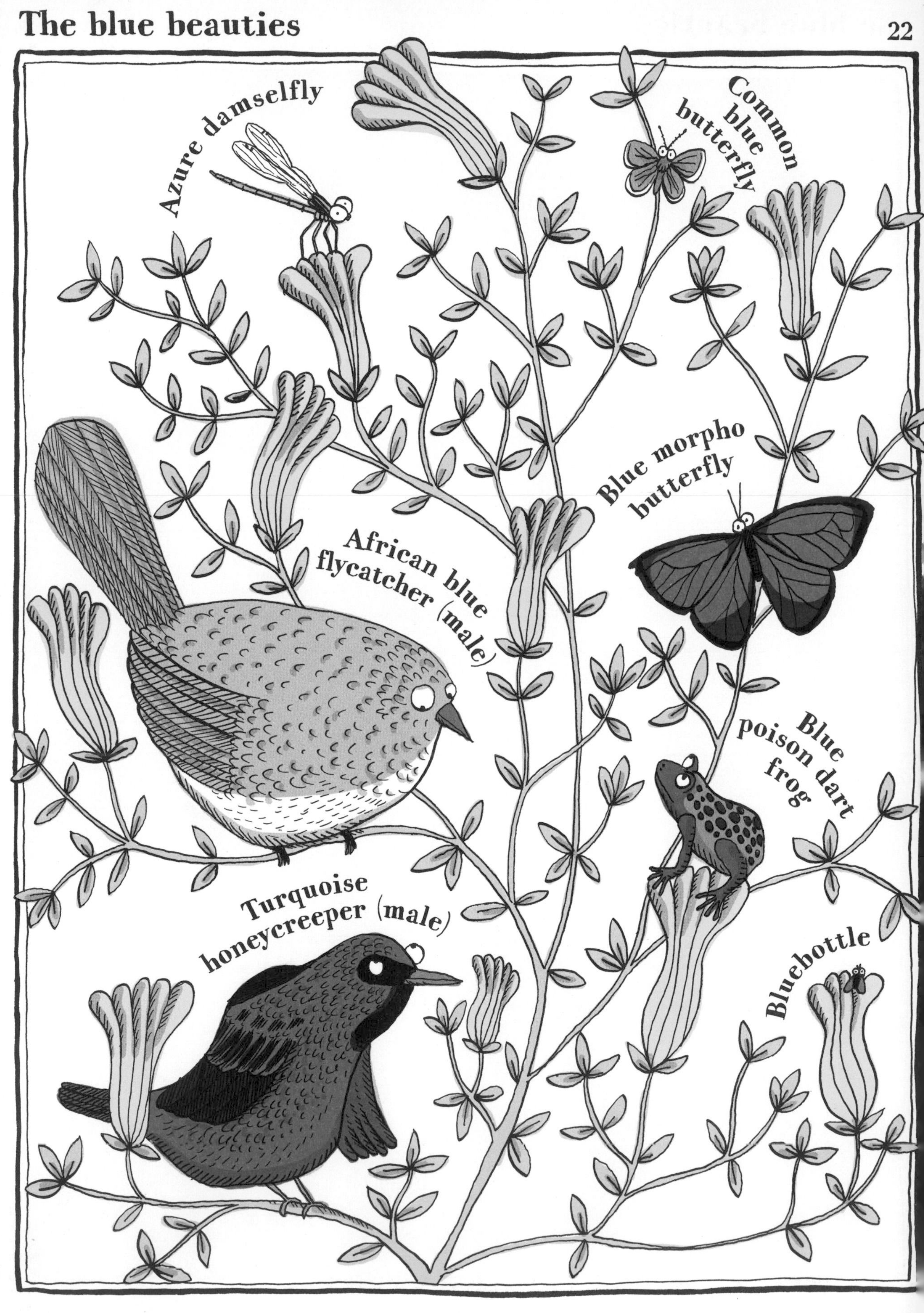

Rainbow agama (male)
Woodland kingfisher
Blue surgeonfish
Blue tit

The bounders

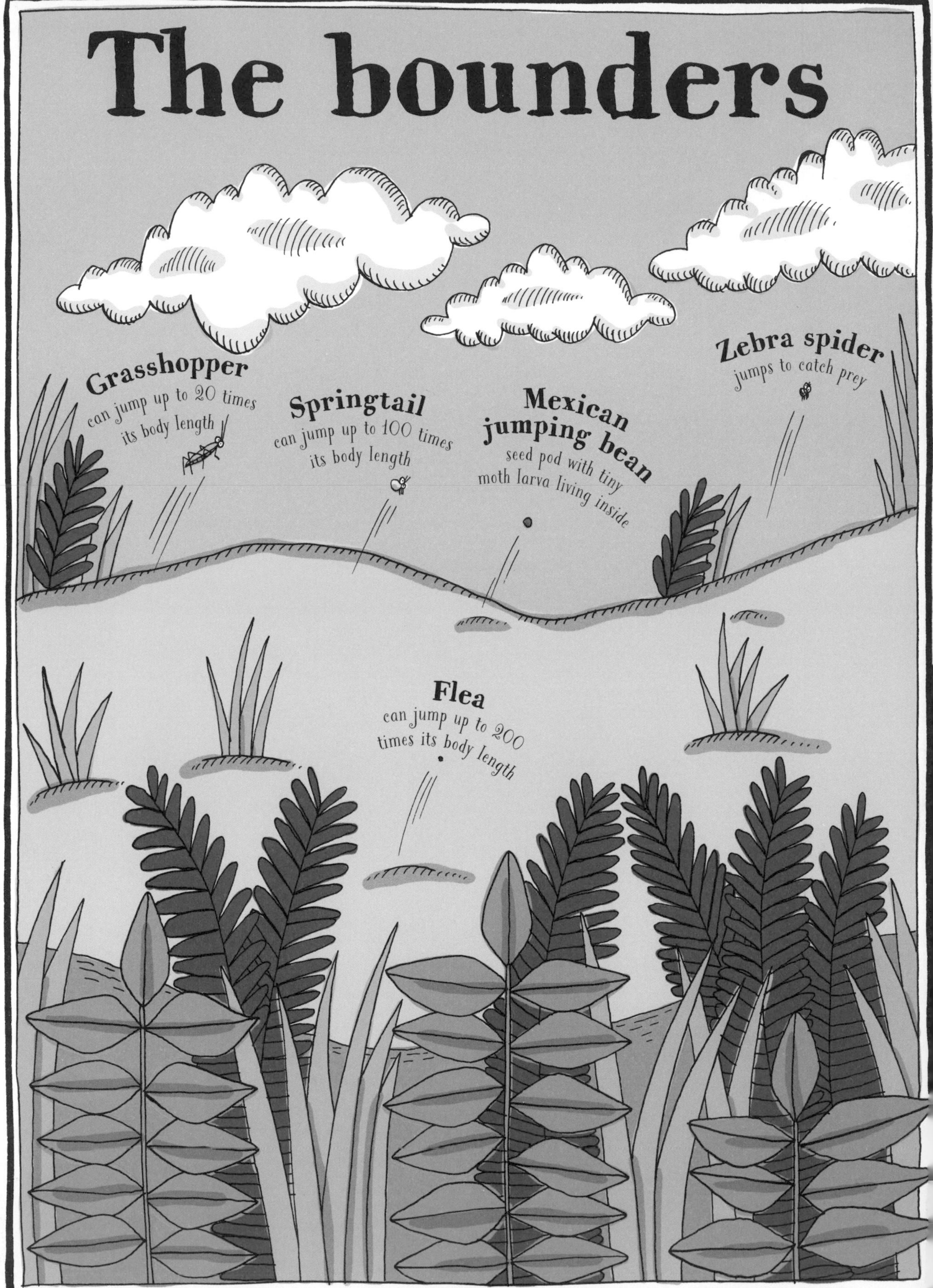

Puma
can leap up to 20 feet from a standing start
Kangaroo
the only large animal that uses jumping as main means of getting around
Flying frog
glides between trees using large webbed feet as parachutes
Atlantic salmon
leaps upstream to get to breeding grounds

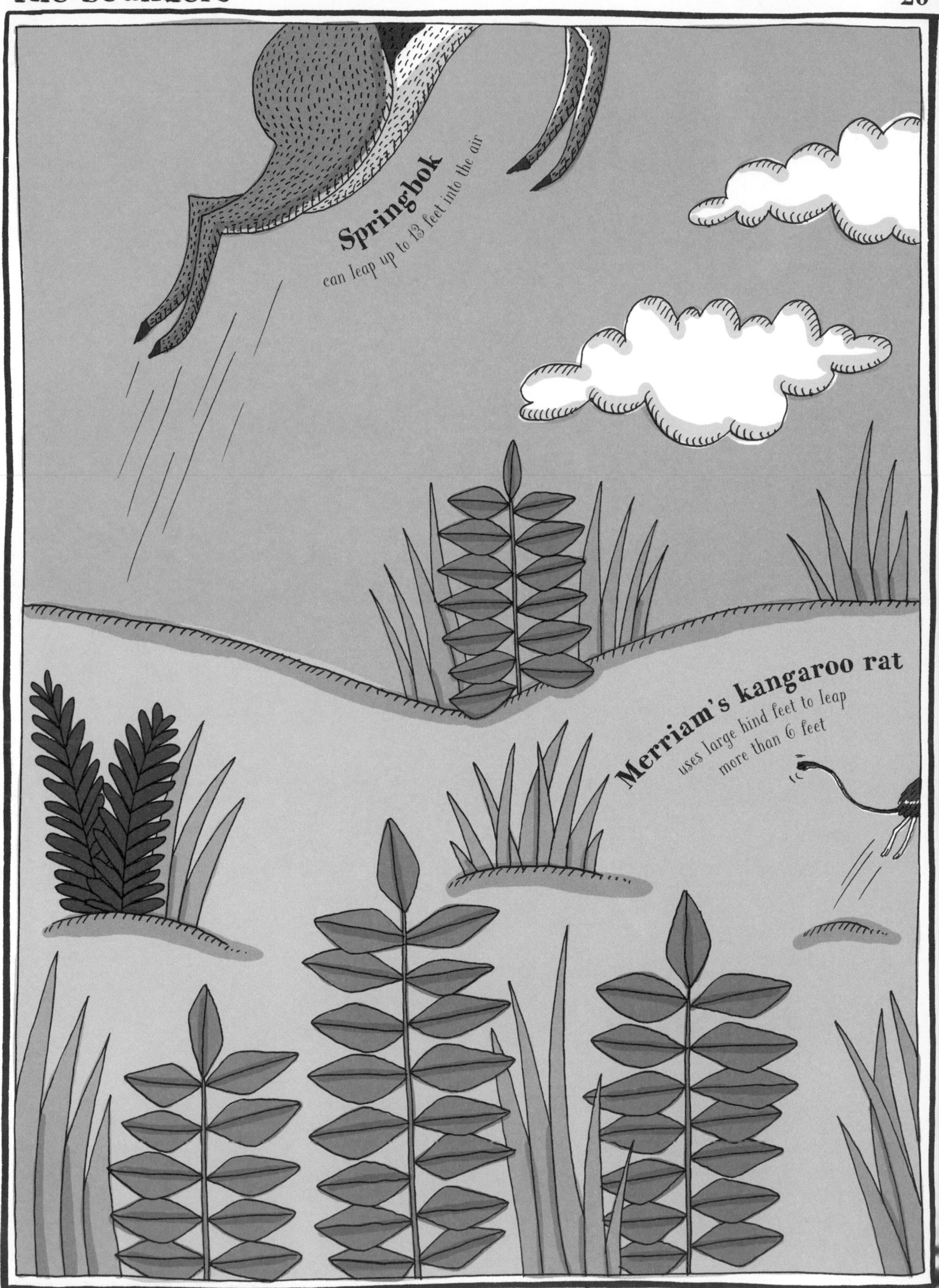
Springbok
can leap up to 13 feet into the air
Merriam's kangaroo rat
uses large hind feet to leap
more than 6 feet

The bounders

Ibex
sure-footed mountain goat;
can jump across crevices
Hare
jumps long distances; can
run at up to 43 mph
Jerboa
can jump up to 10 feet

The brainboxes

Chimpanzee
good at problem-solving
Parakeet
recognizes colors, shapes, and numbers
good memory
makes and uses tools
self-aware
Jungle crow

Common octopus
good memory
quick learner
uses tools
Rat
swarm intelligence
Common wasp
episodic memory

Dolphin
self-aware
Honeybee
sense of direction
swarm intelligence
Red wood ant

The canary-yellows
Blue-cheeked butterfly fish

Yellow
meadow ant
Common
brimstone
butterfly
Banana
slug
Twenty-
two-spot
ladybug
Owly
sulphur

American
yellow
warbler
Kinkajou
Golden oriole
(male)
Pumpkin toadlet
Pineapplefish

The champion breath-holders

Walrus 30 minutes

The champion breath-holders

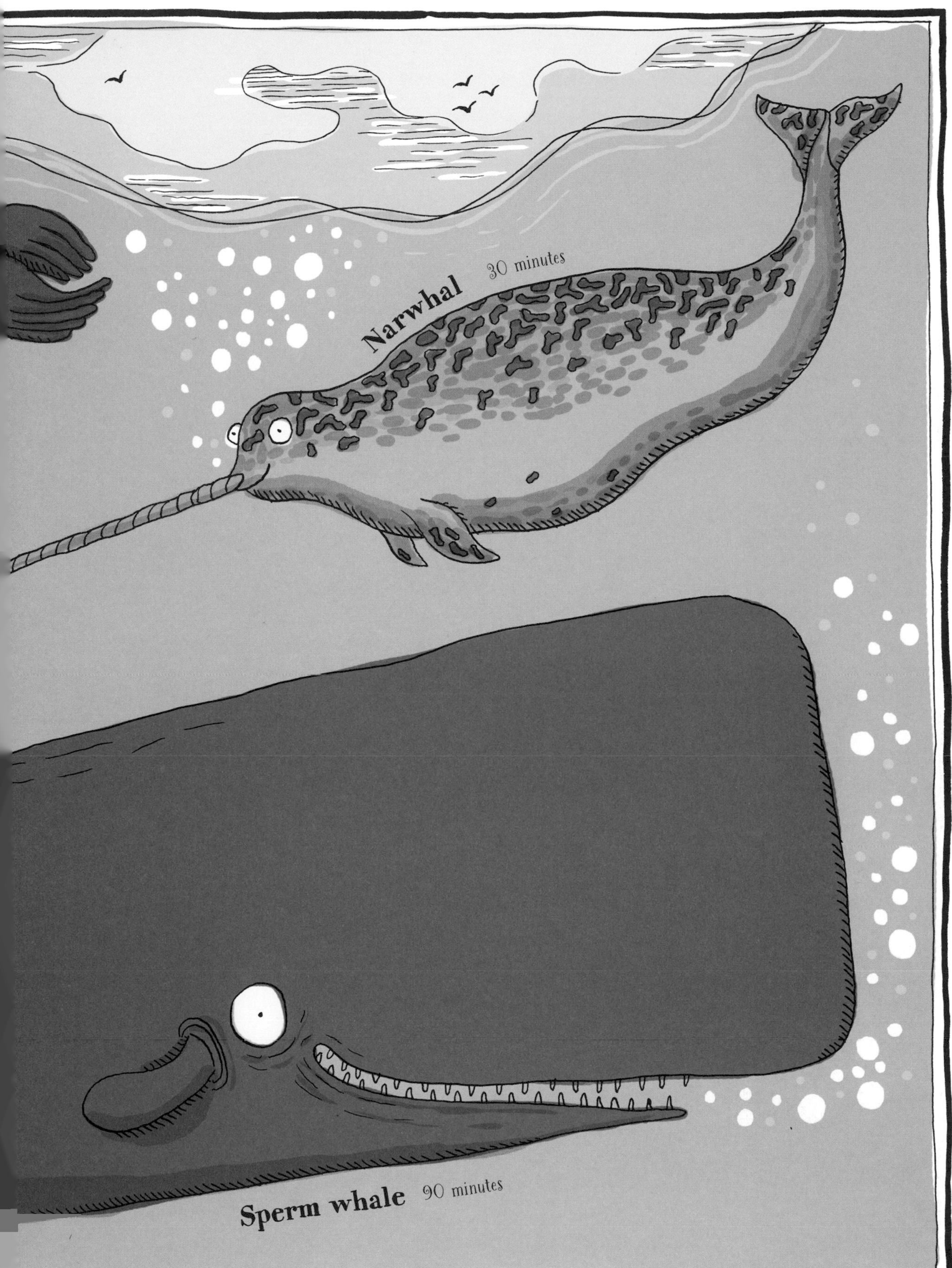
Narwhal 30 minutes
Sperm whale 90 minutes

Hippopotamus
5 minutes

Alligator snapping turtle
40-50 minutes
American alligator
60 minutes

The coal-blacks

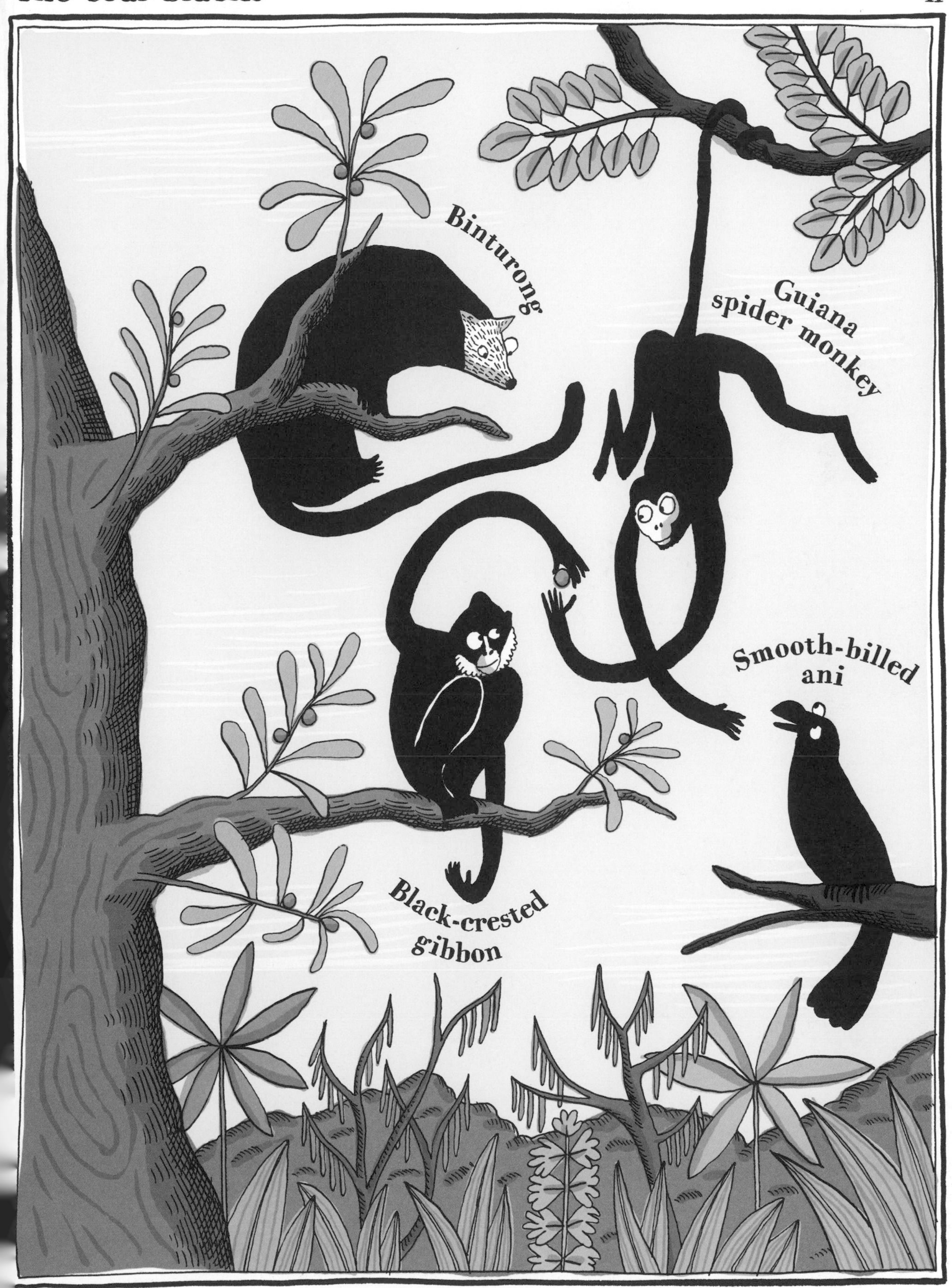
Binturong
Guiana spider monkey
Smooth-billed ani
Black-crested gibbon

Black bear
Capricorn beetle
Violet ground beetle

Black panther
Black ant
Dung beetle

Black salamander
Common blackbird
Mexican black king snake

The endangered

Giant panda

Orangutan
Green mantella
Lear's macaw
Blobfish
Markhor
White-rumped vulture

Southern cassowary

Saw-tailed bush cricket

Hawaiian monk seal

Drill

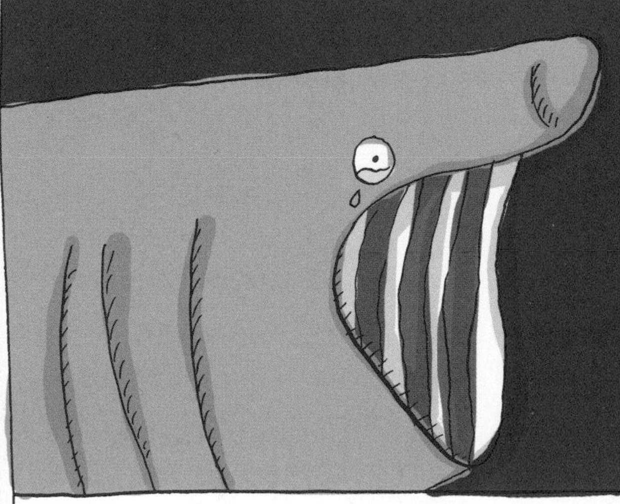
Basking shark

Chuckwalla

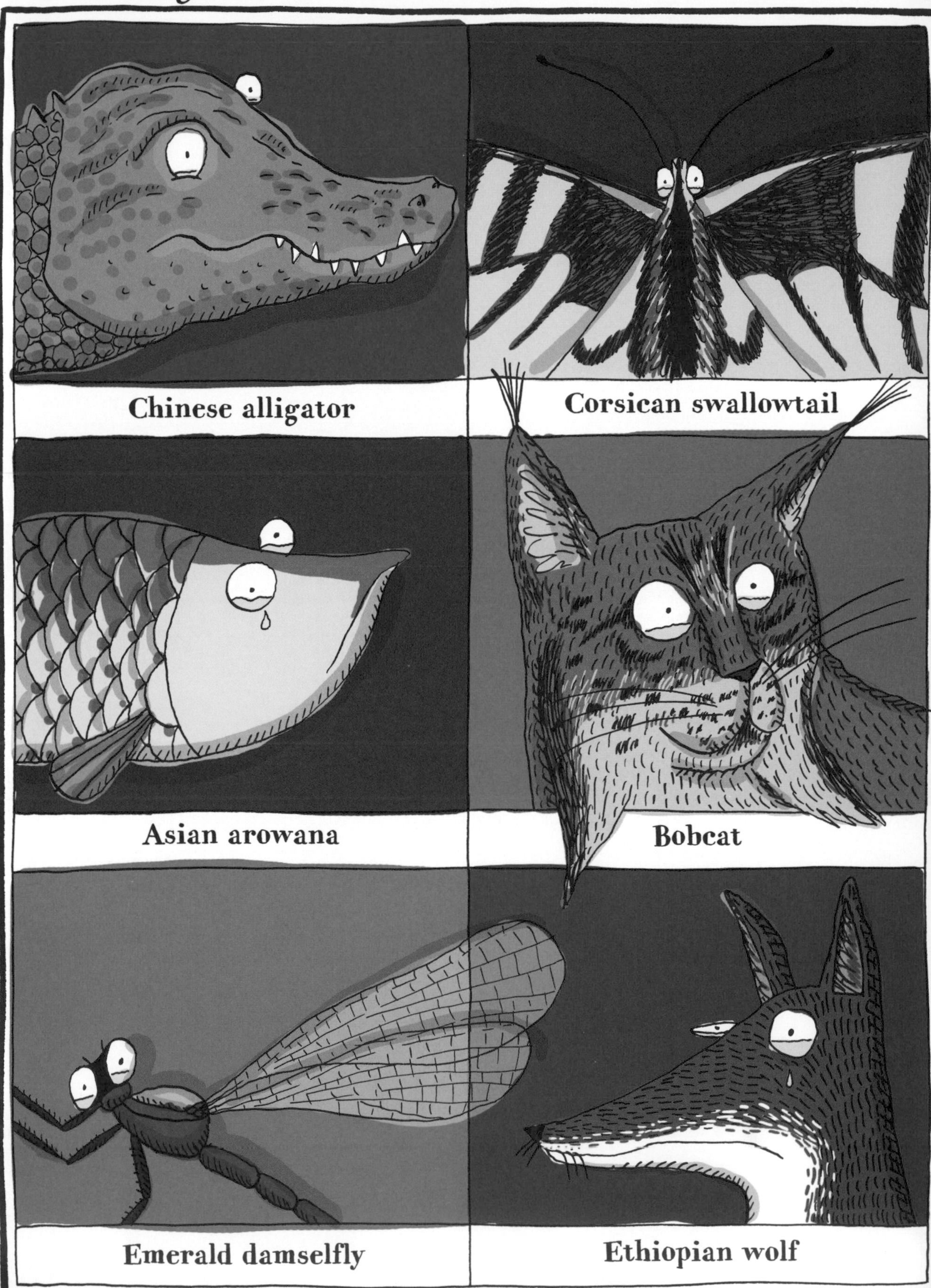
Chinese alligator
Corsican swallowtail
Asian arowana
Bobcat
Emerald damselfly
Ethiopian wolf

Snow leopard

Golden lion tamarin

Monkey-eating eagle

Hermit beetle

Green sea turtle

Otter

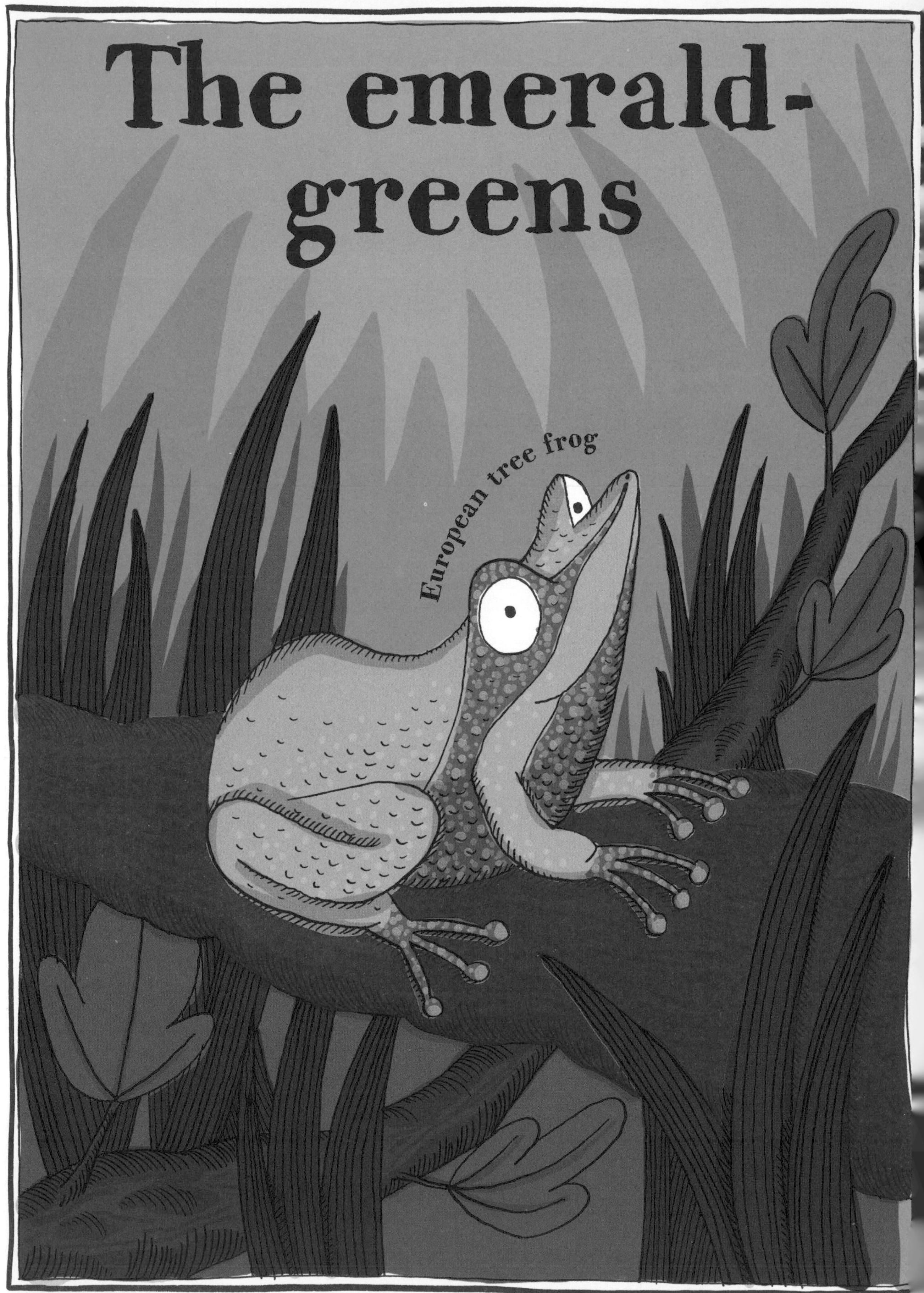
The emerald-greens
European tree frog

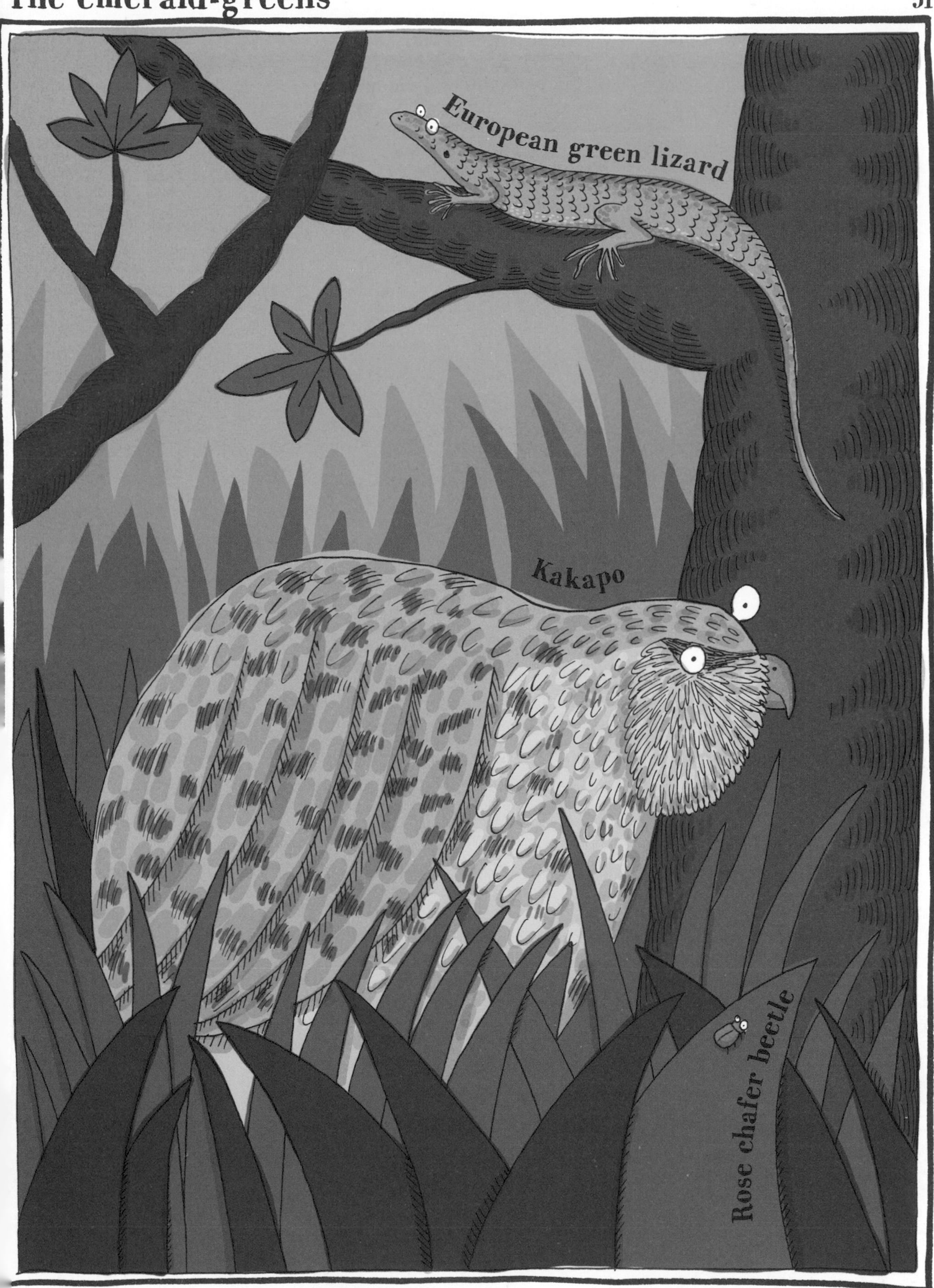
European green lizard
Kakapo
Rose chafer beetle

Green anole
Rose-ringed parakeet
Green hairstreak butterfly
Green mamba
Plumed basilisk

Emerald toucanet
Greenbottle
Emerald tree boa
Green tiger beetle
Green broadbill
Green shield bug

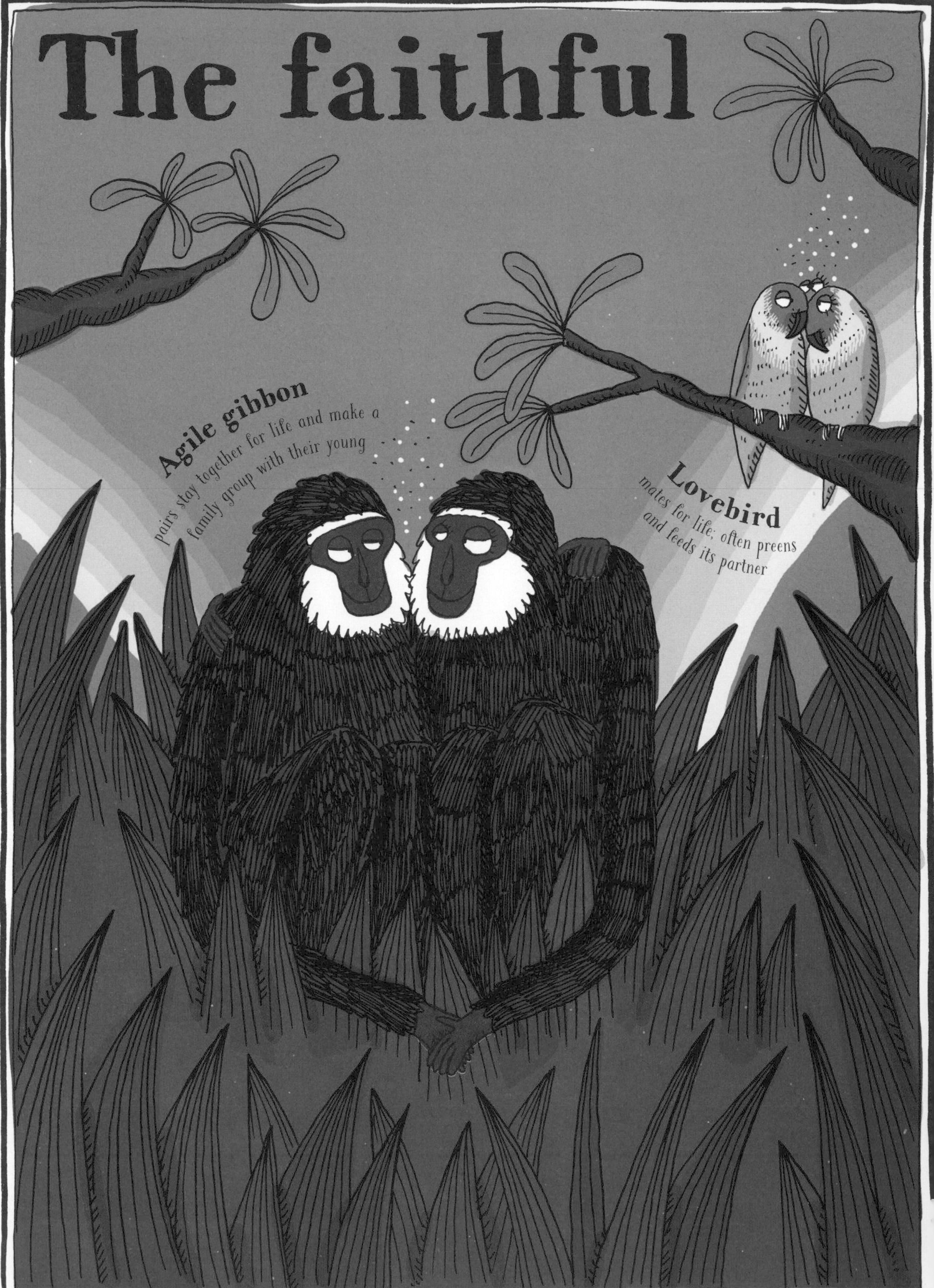

The faithful
Agile gibbon
pairs stay together for life and make a
family group with their young
Lovebird
mates for life; often preens
and feeds its partner

Dik-dik
pairs mate for life
and are rarely seen apart
Mongolian gerbil
Wandering albatross
Whooper swan
Sea horse
Mandarin duck

Common crane
pairs make bonds that may last whole lives
Corsac fox
males help care for the young
Patagonian mara

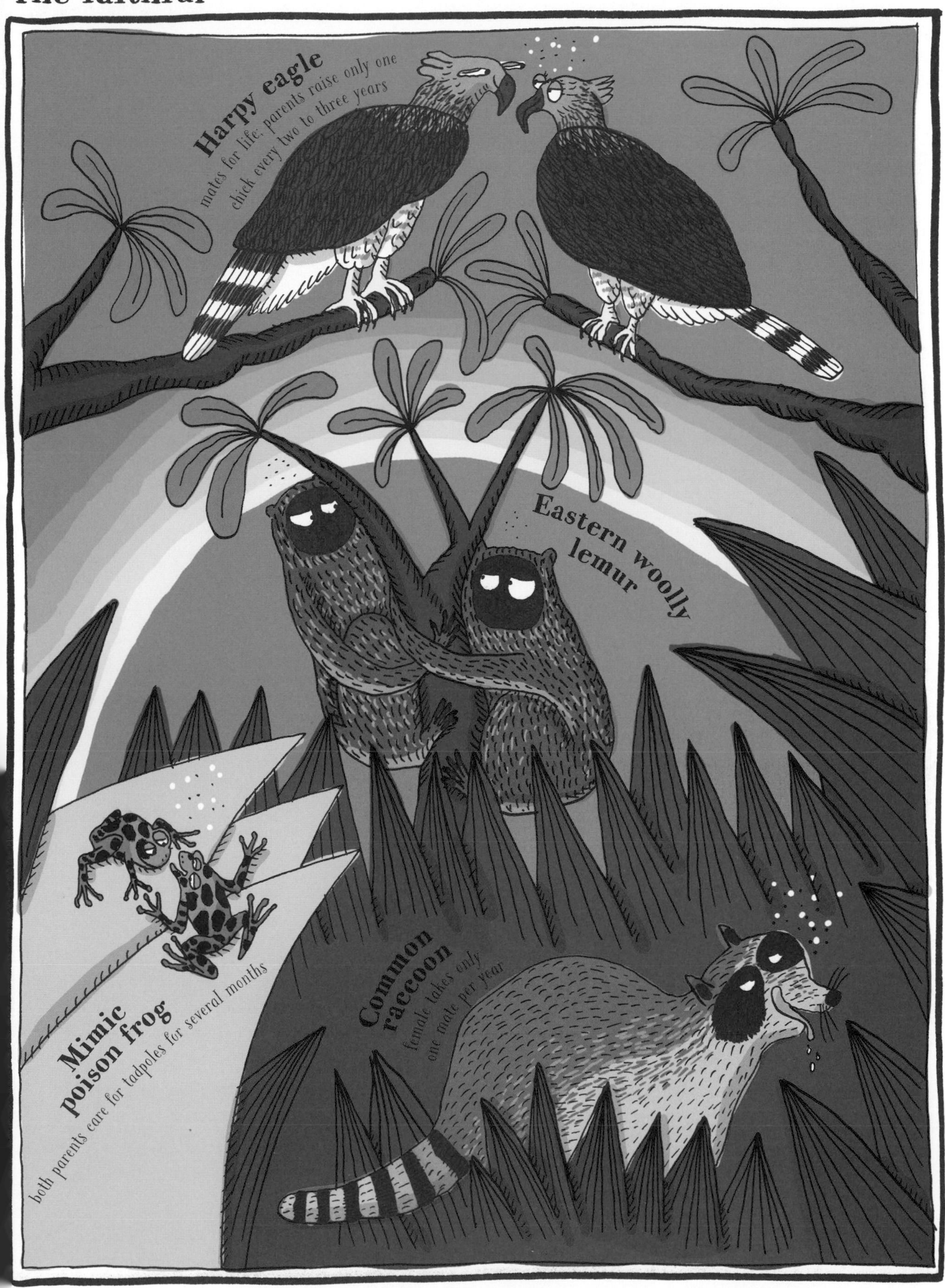
Harpy eagle
mates for life; parents raise only one chick every two to three years
Eastern woolly lemur
Mimic poison frog
both parents care for tadpoles for several months
Common raccoon
female takes only one mate per year

Our family friends

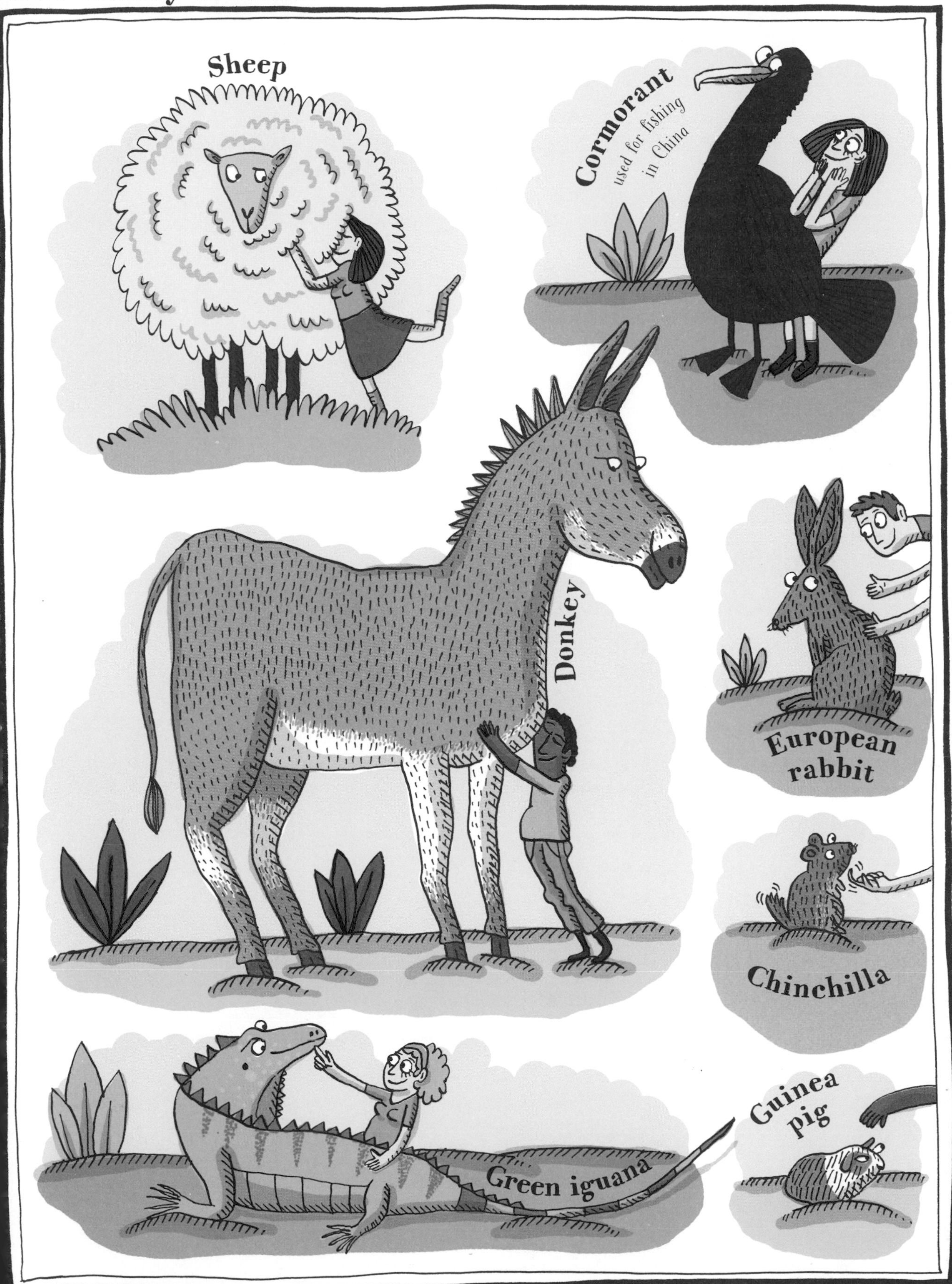
Sheep
Cormorant
used for fishing
in China
Donkey
European
rabbit
Chinchilla
Green iguana
Guinea
pig

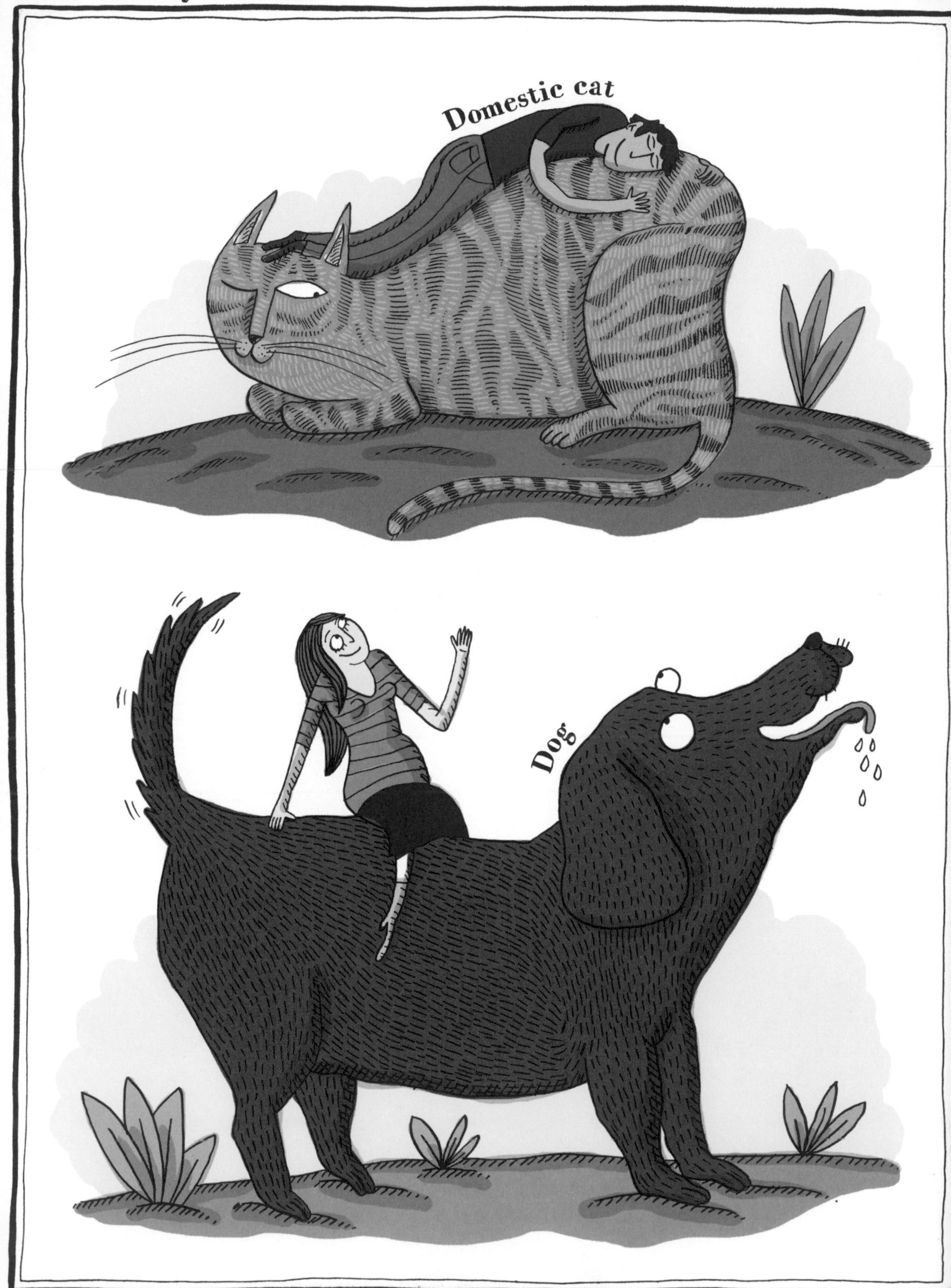
Domestic cat
Dog

Goat
Llama
used for transport and wool
Cow
Water buffalo
used to plow fields, and for milk

Horse
Camel

Ferret
Budgerigar
Hamster
Domestic mouse
Frog
Snake
Hermit crab
Goldfish
Canary
Congo tetra

The fierce

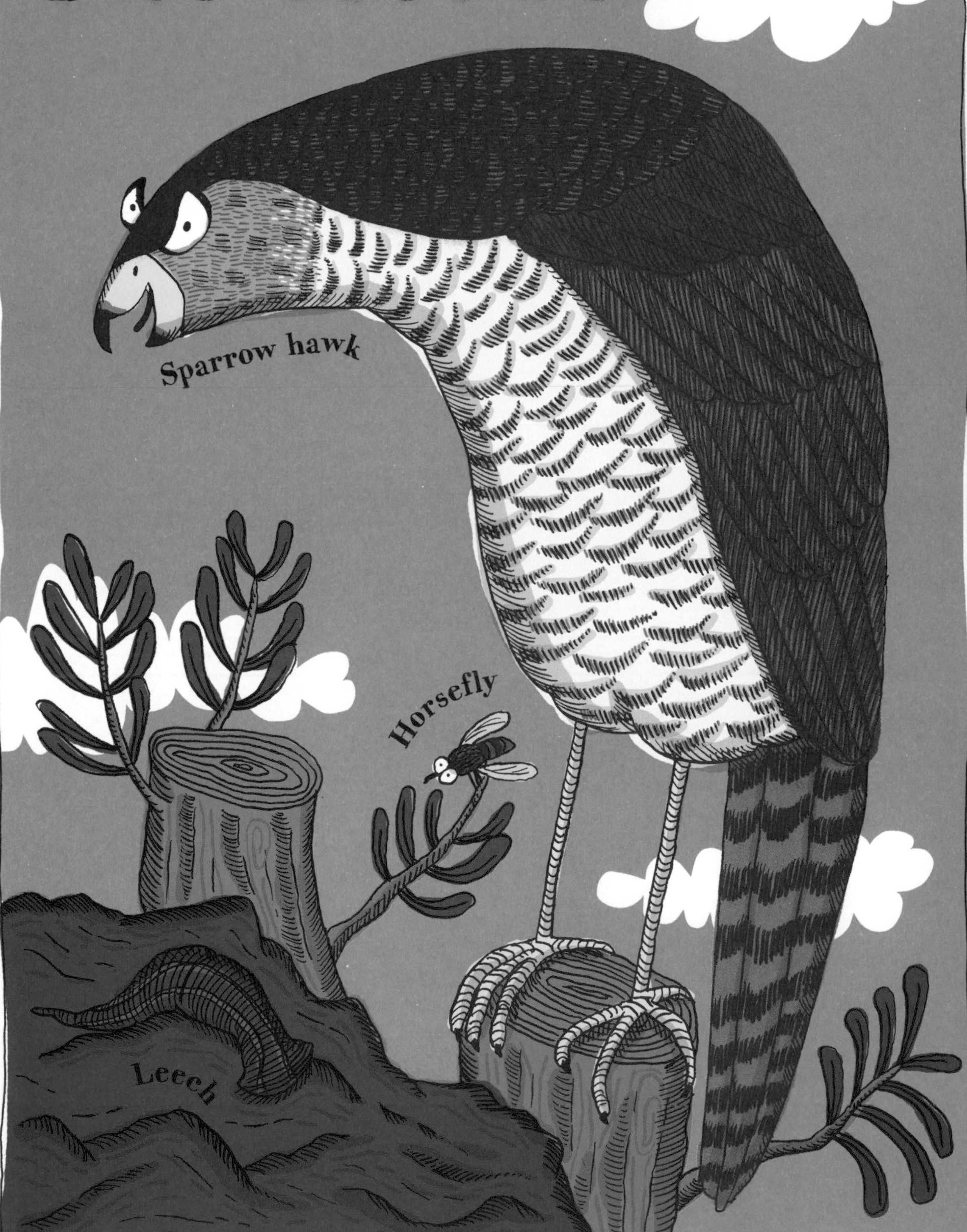
Sparrow hawk
Horsefly
Leech

Olive baboon
Asian hornet
Mosquito
Tasmanian devil

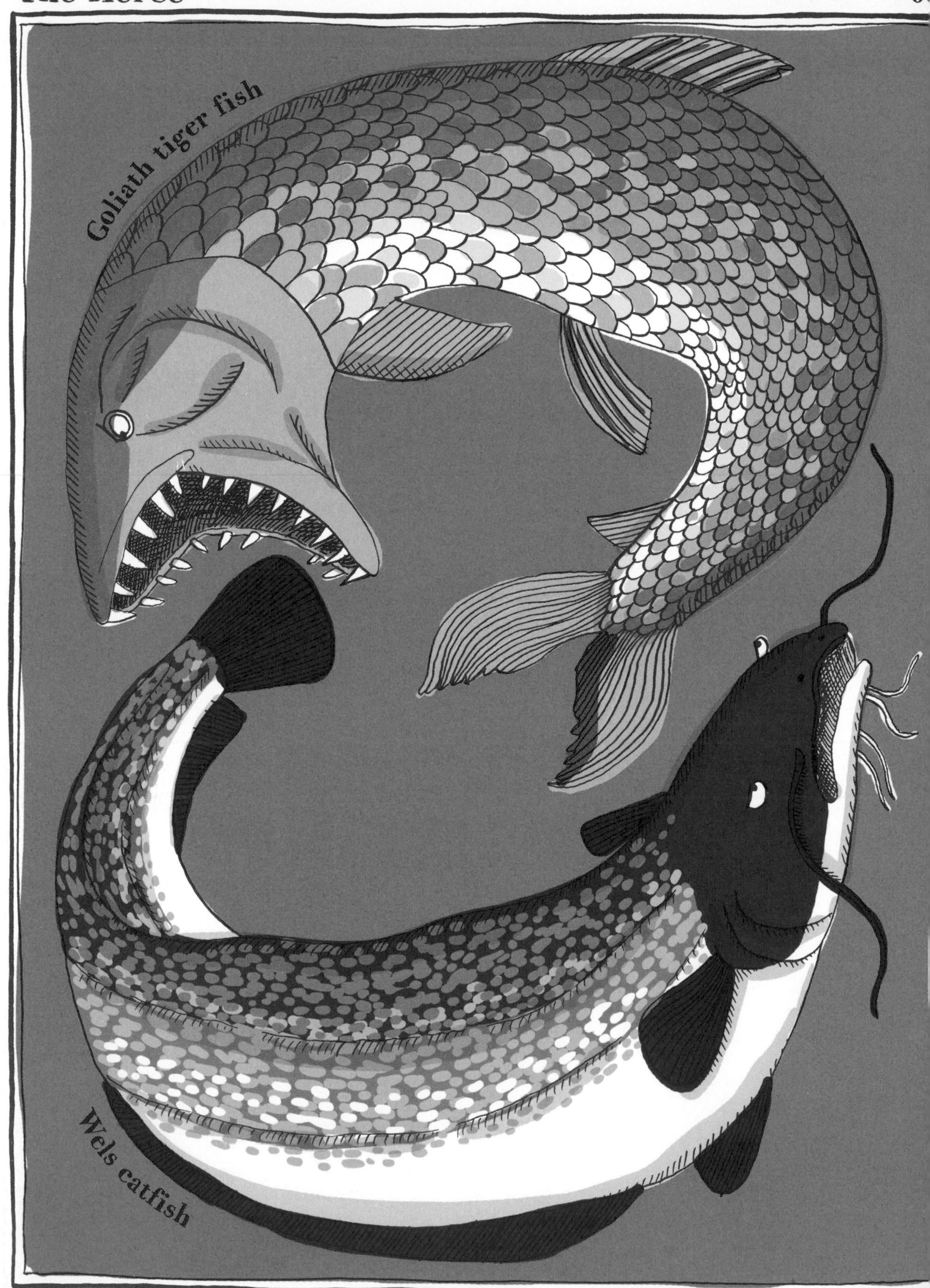
Goliath tiger fish
Wels catfish

Tick
Grizzly bear
Stoat

Kestrel
Inland taipan

Tiger shark
Asiatic softshell turtle

The foresters

Indri
Loris
Grove snail
Red squirrel

Emerald tree monitor
Edible dormouse
Valerio's glass frog
Sable

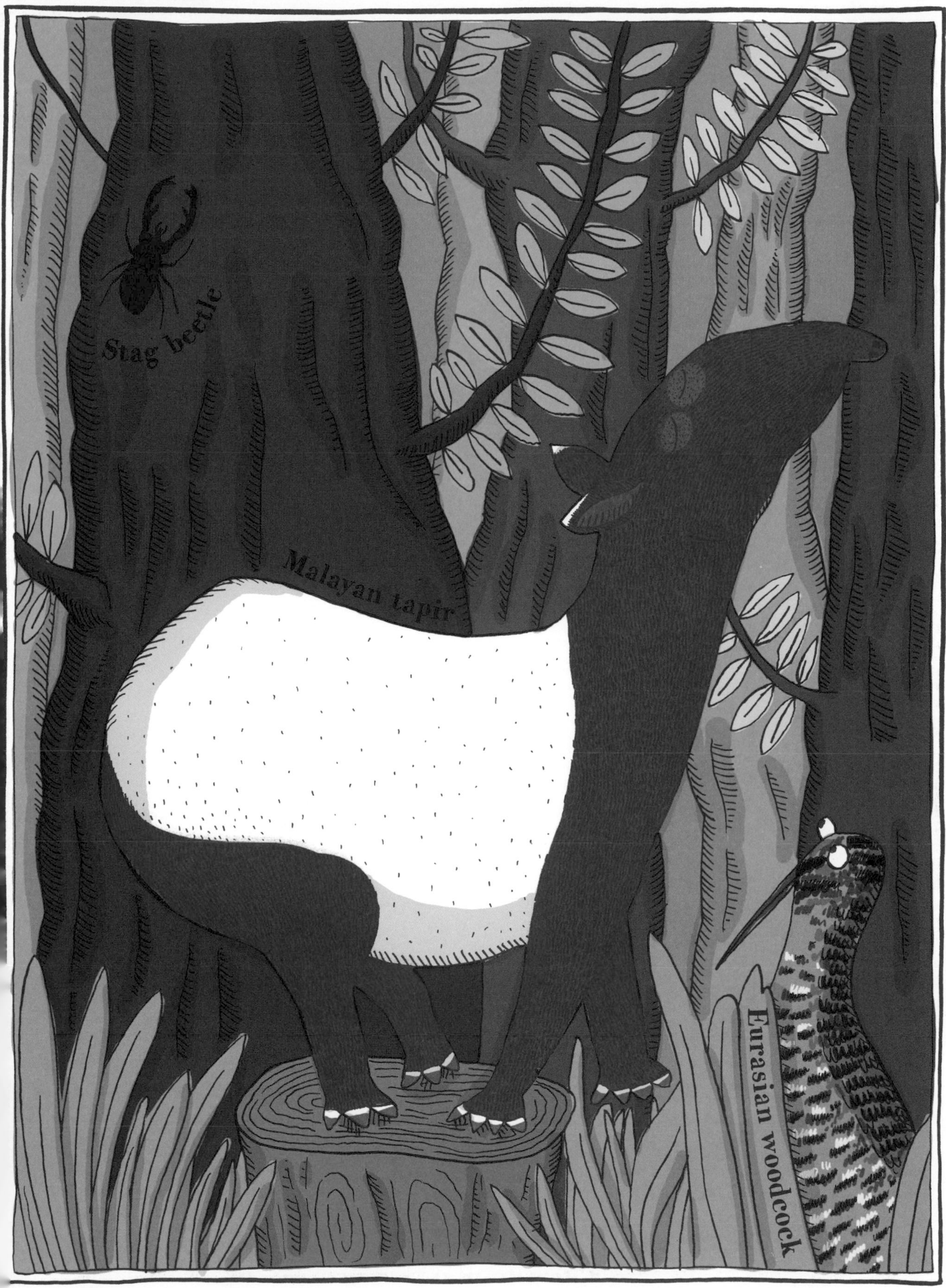
Stag beetle
Malayan tapir
Eurasian woodcock

Hawfinch
Brown greater galago
Babirusa

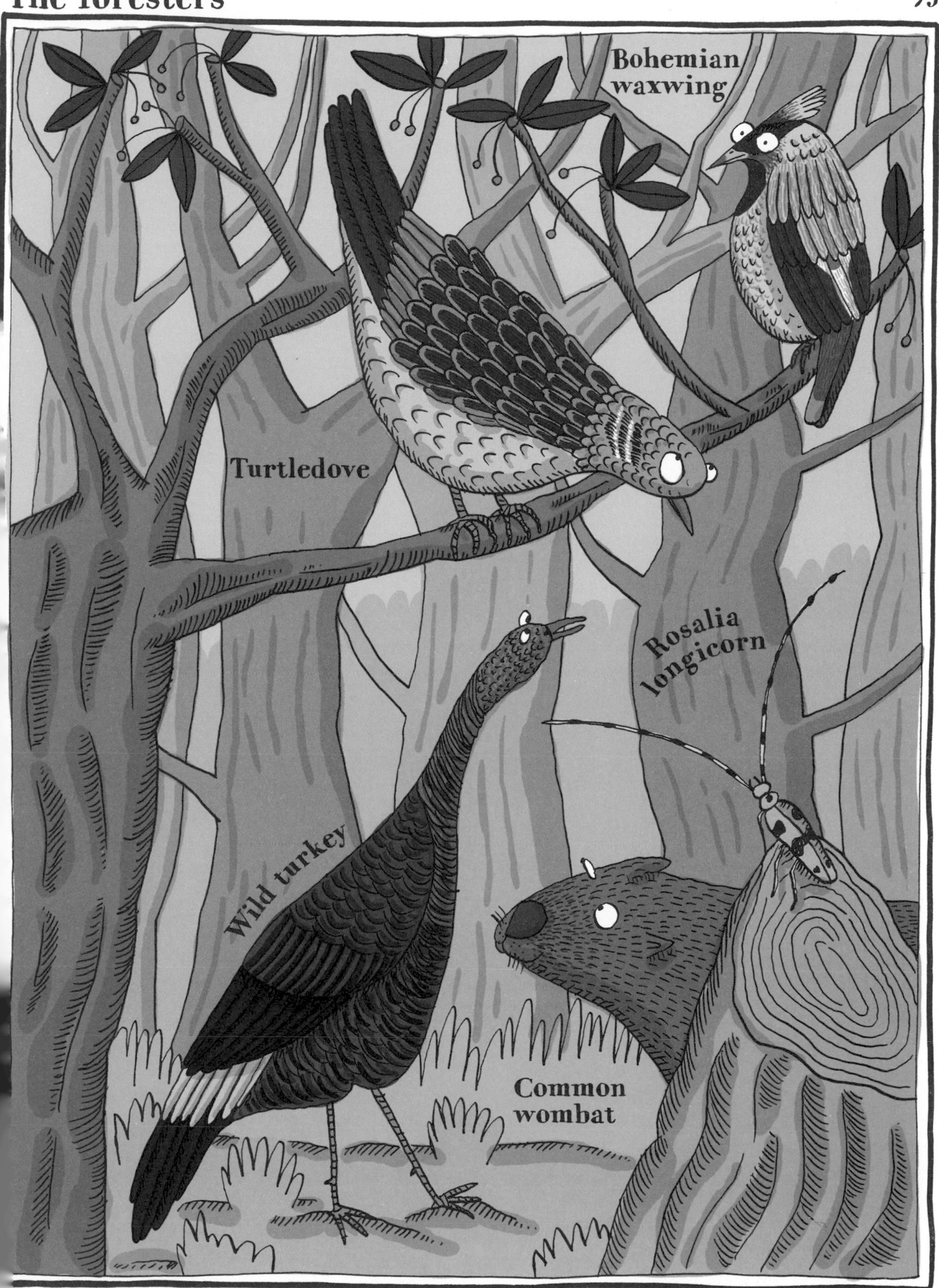
Bohemian
waxwing
Turtledove
Rosalia
longicorn
Wild turkey
Common
wombat

The giants
Giant Pacific octopus
world's largest octopus: up to 30 feet across

The giants

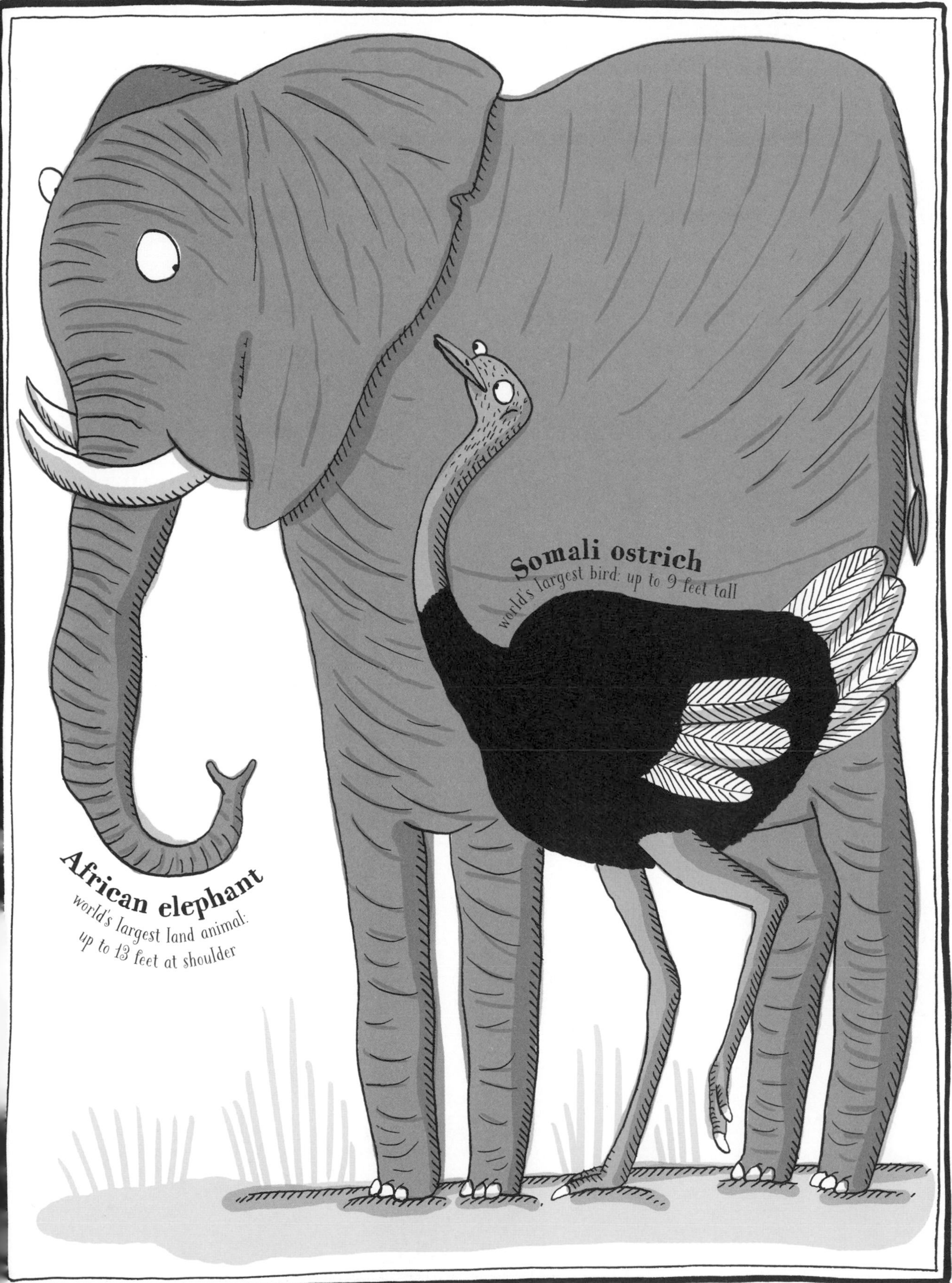

Somali ostrich
world's largest bird: up to 9 feet tall
African elephant
world's largest land animal:
up to 13 feet at shoulder

Goliath bird-eating spider
up to 11-inch legspan
Goliath frog
world's largest frog: up to 13 inches long
Chinese giant salamander
world's largest amphibian: up to 6 feet long

Japanese spider crab
up to 12-foot legspan
Giant Gippsland earthworm
up to 10 feet long
Arapaima
up to 8 feet long

The giants

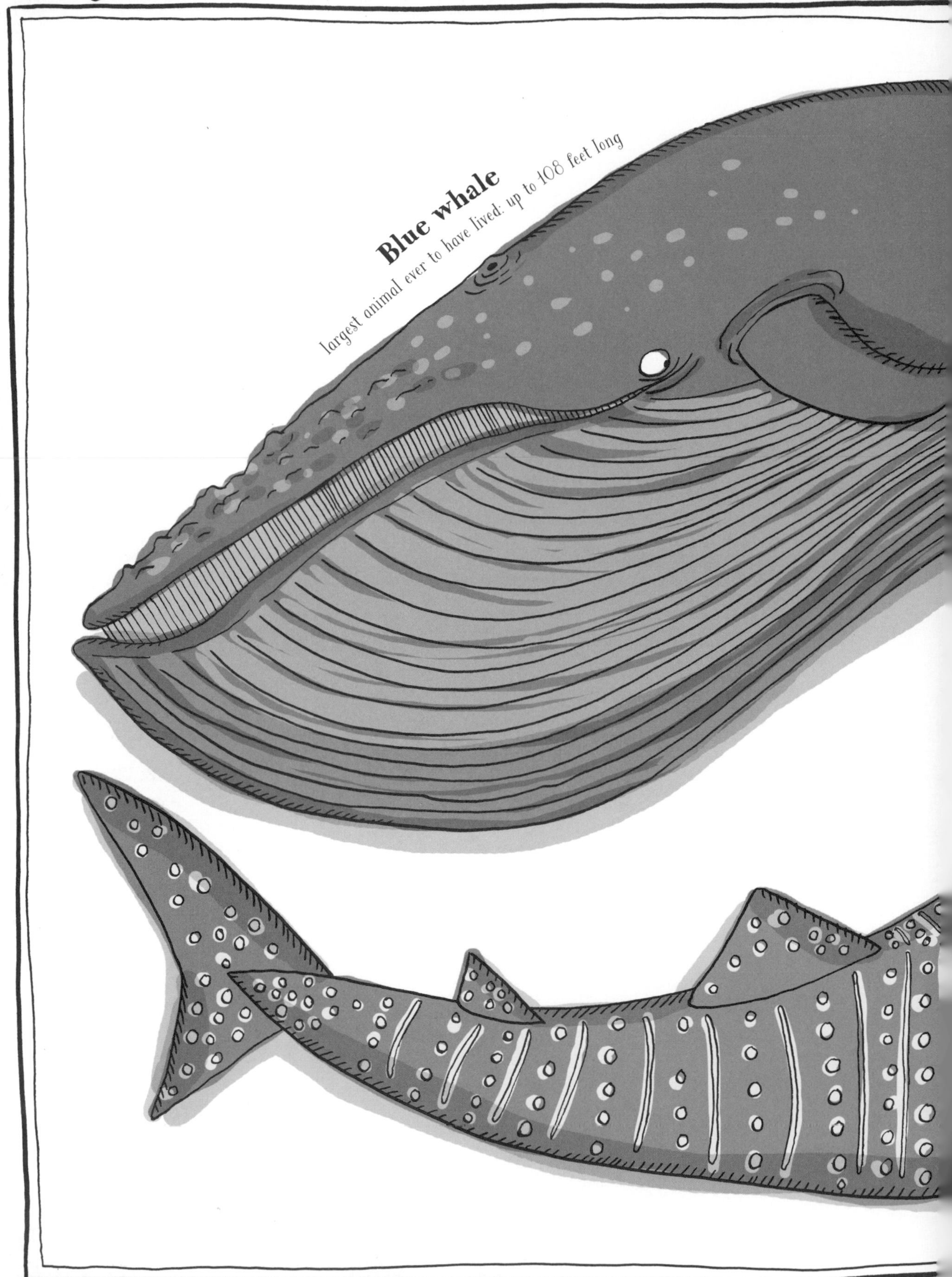

Blue whale
largest animal ever to have lived: up to 108 feet long

Whale shark
world's largest fish: up to 40 feet long

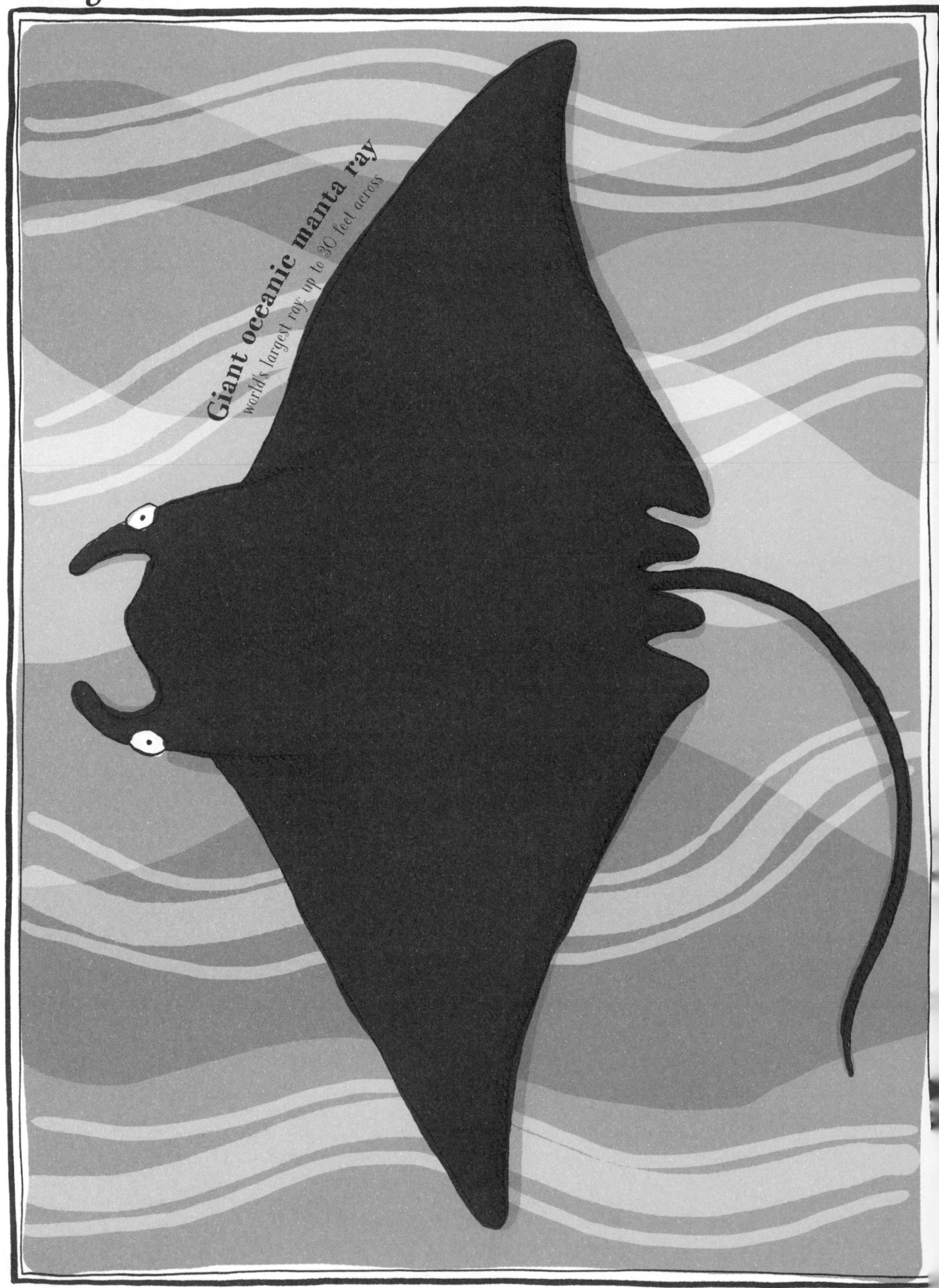
Giant oceanic manta ray
world's largest ray: up to 30 feet across

Titan beetle
up to 6.5 inches long
Capybara
world's largest rodent: up to 4 feet long
Gorilla
world's largest primate: up to 6 feet tall

The giants

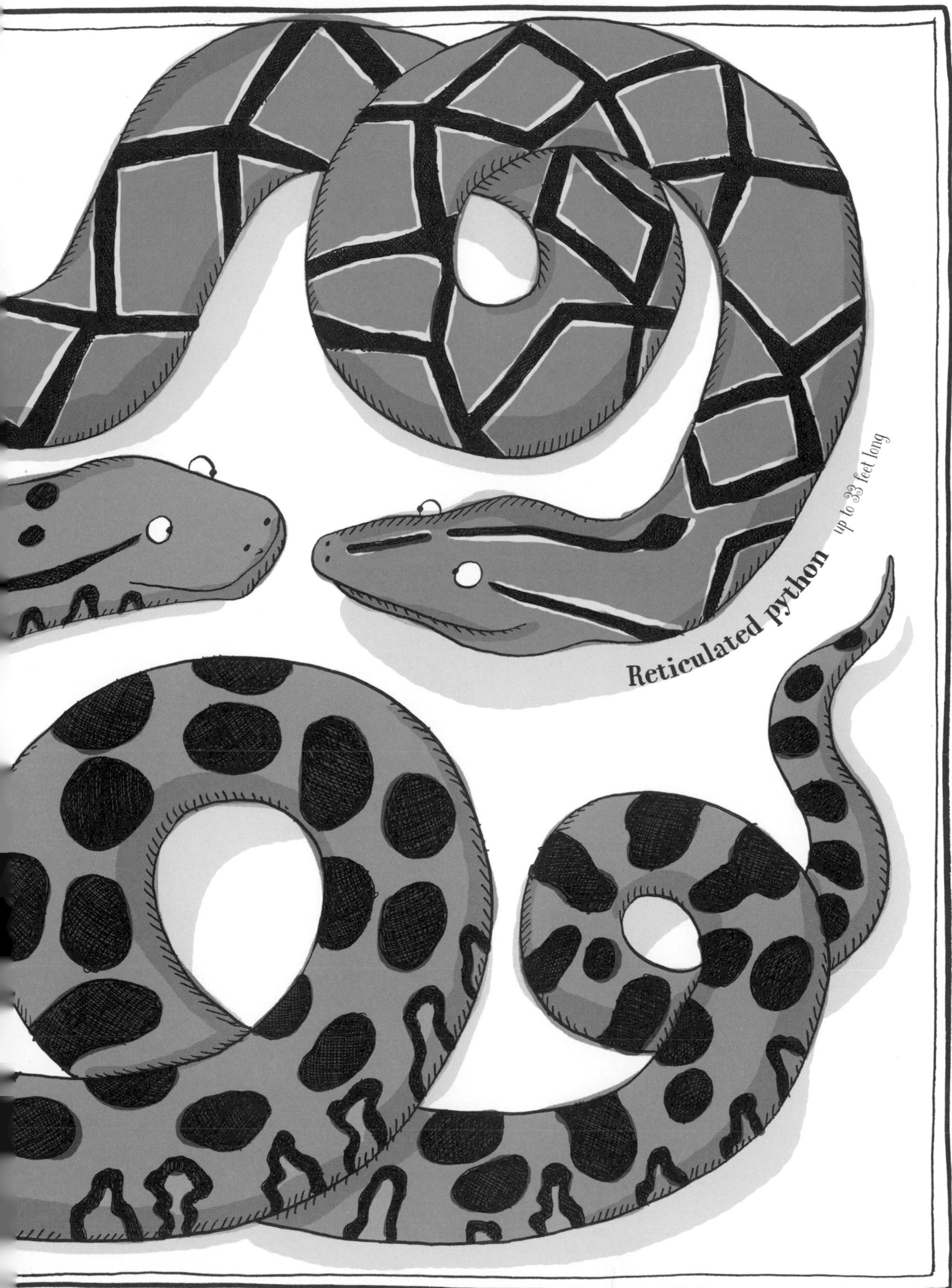
Reticulated python
up to 33 feet long

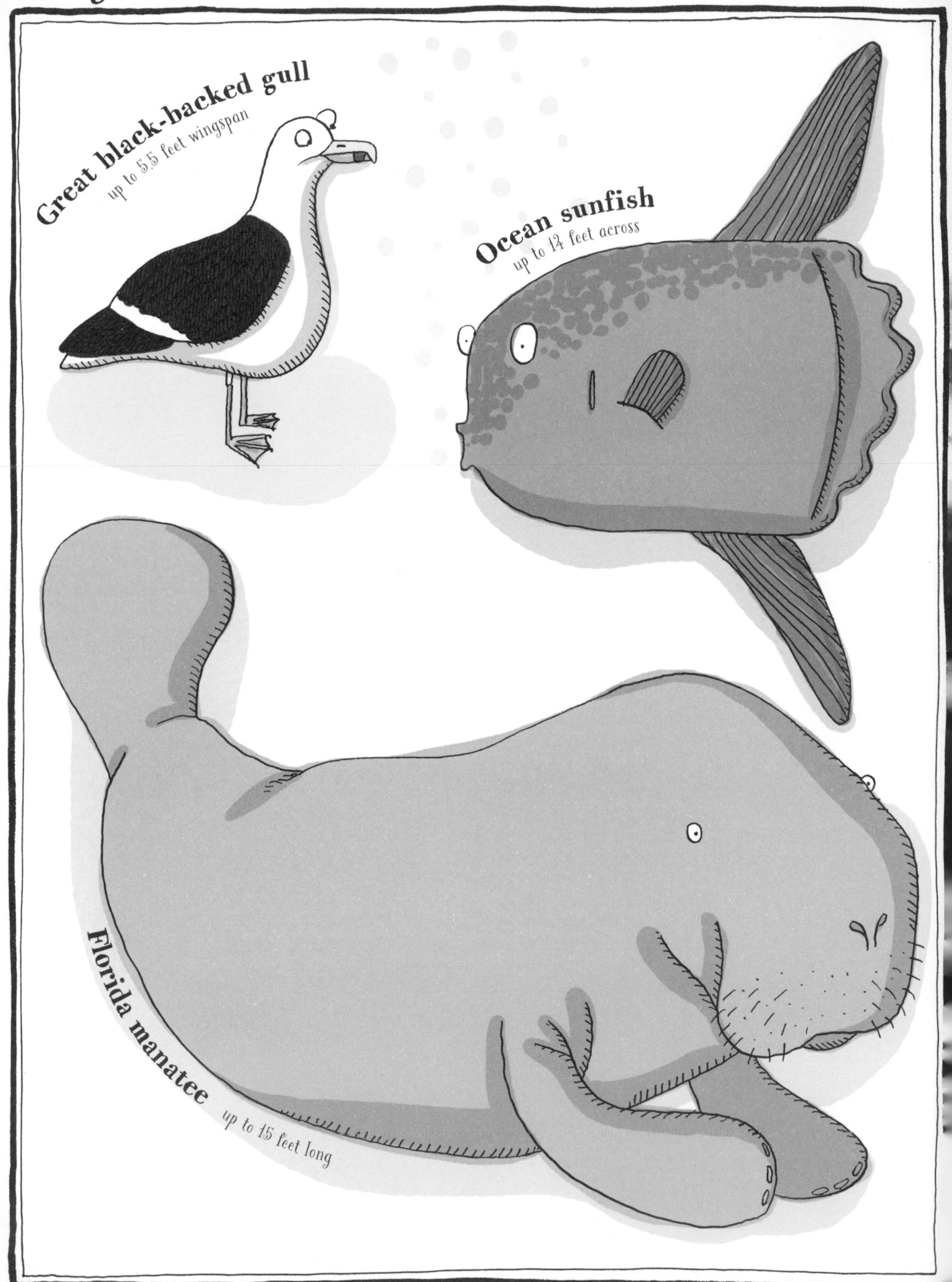
Great black-backed gull
up to 5.5 feet wingspan
Ocean sunfish
up to 14 feet across
Florida manatee
up to 15 feet long

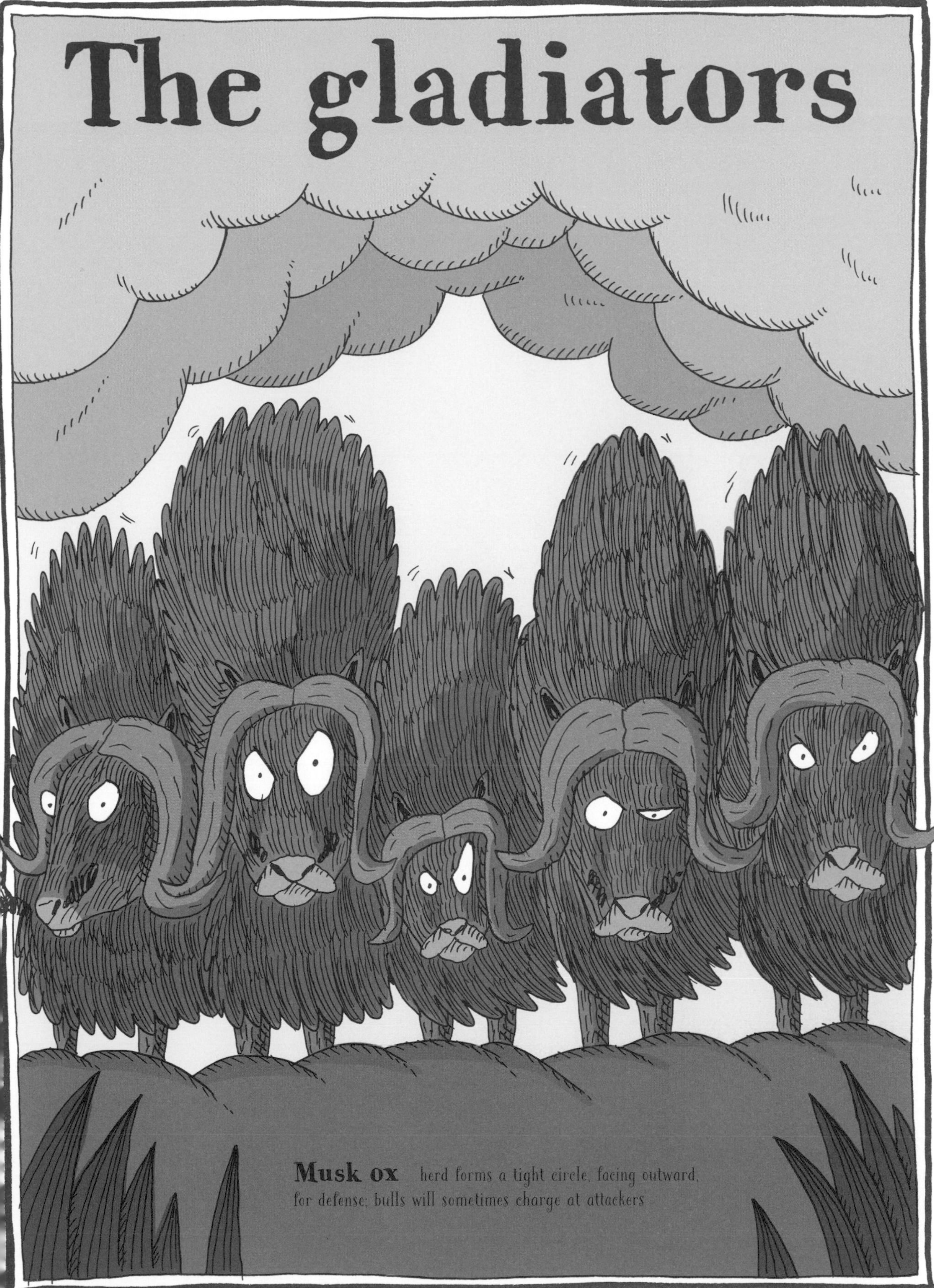
The gladiators
Musk ox herd forms a tight circle, facing outward, for defense; bulls will sometimes charge at attackers

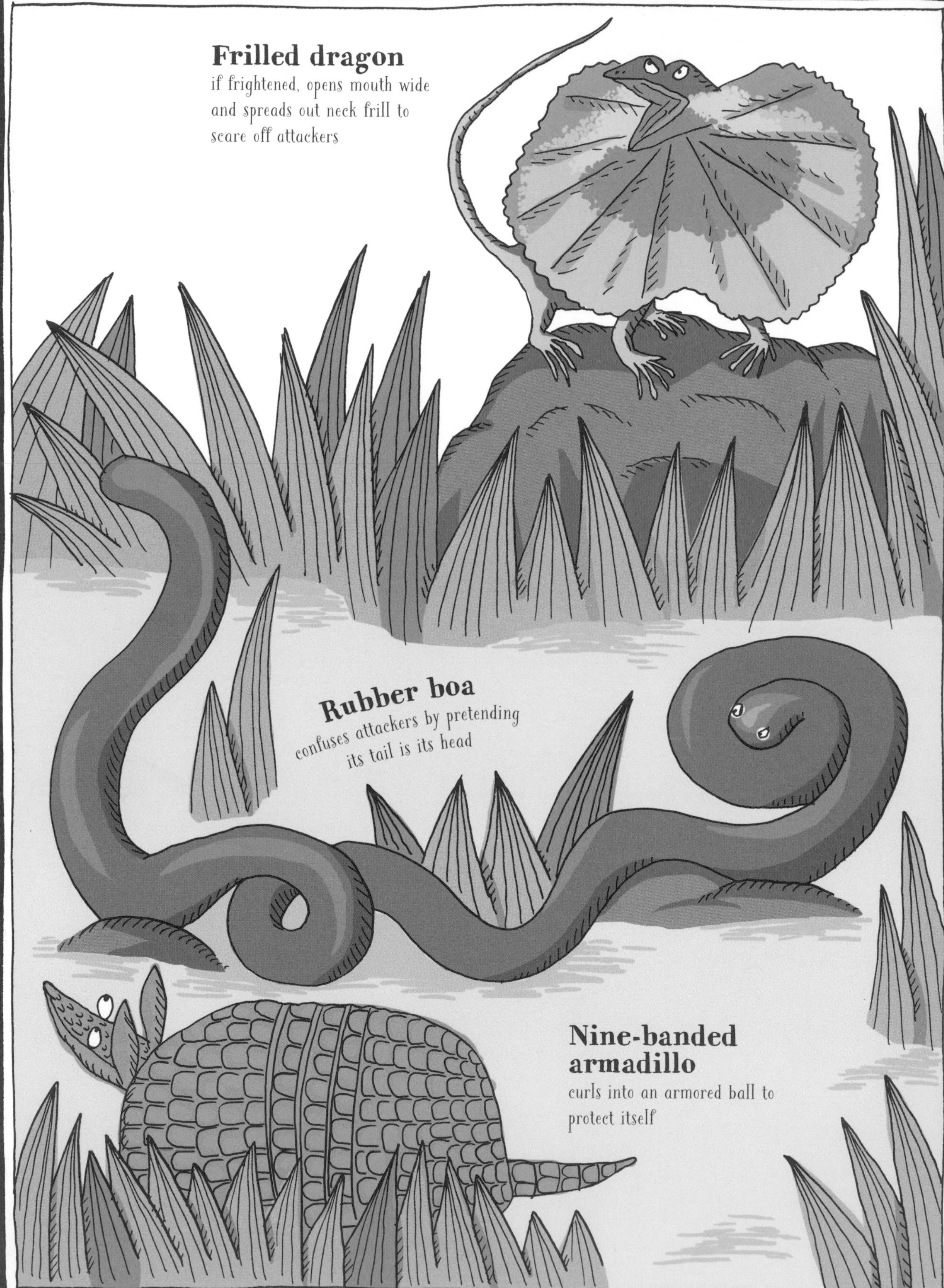
Frilled dragon
if frightened, opens mouth wide and spreads out neck frill to scare off attackers
Rubber boa
confuses attackers by pretending its tail is its head
Nine-banded armadillo
curls into an armored ball to protect itself

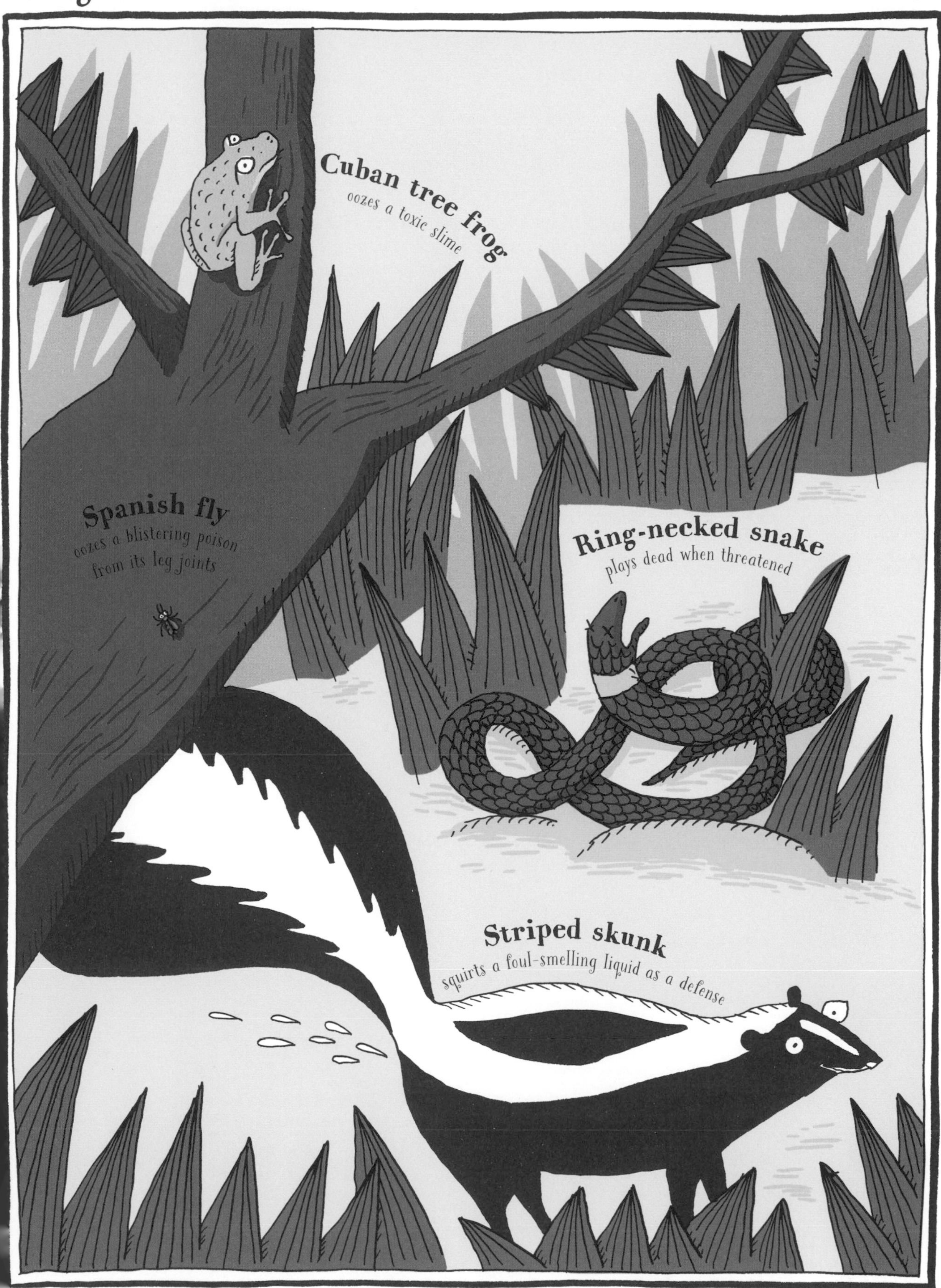
Cuban tree frog
oozes a toxic slime
Spanish fly
oozes a blistering poison
from its leg joints
Ring-necked snake
plays dead when threatened
Striped skunk
squirts a foul-smelling liquid as a defense

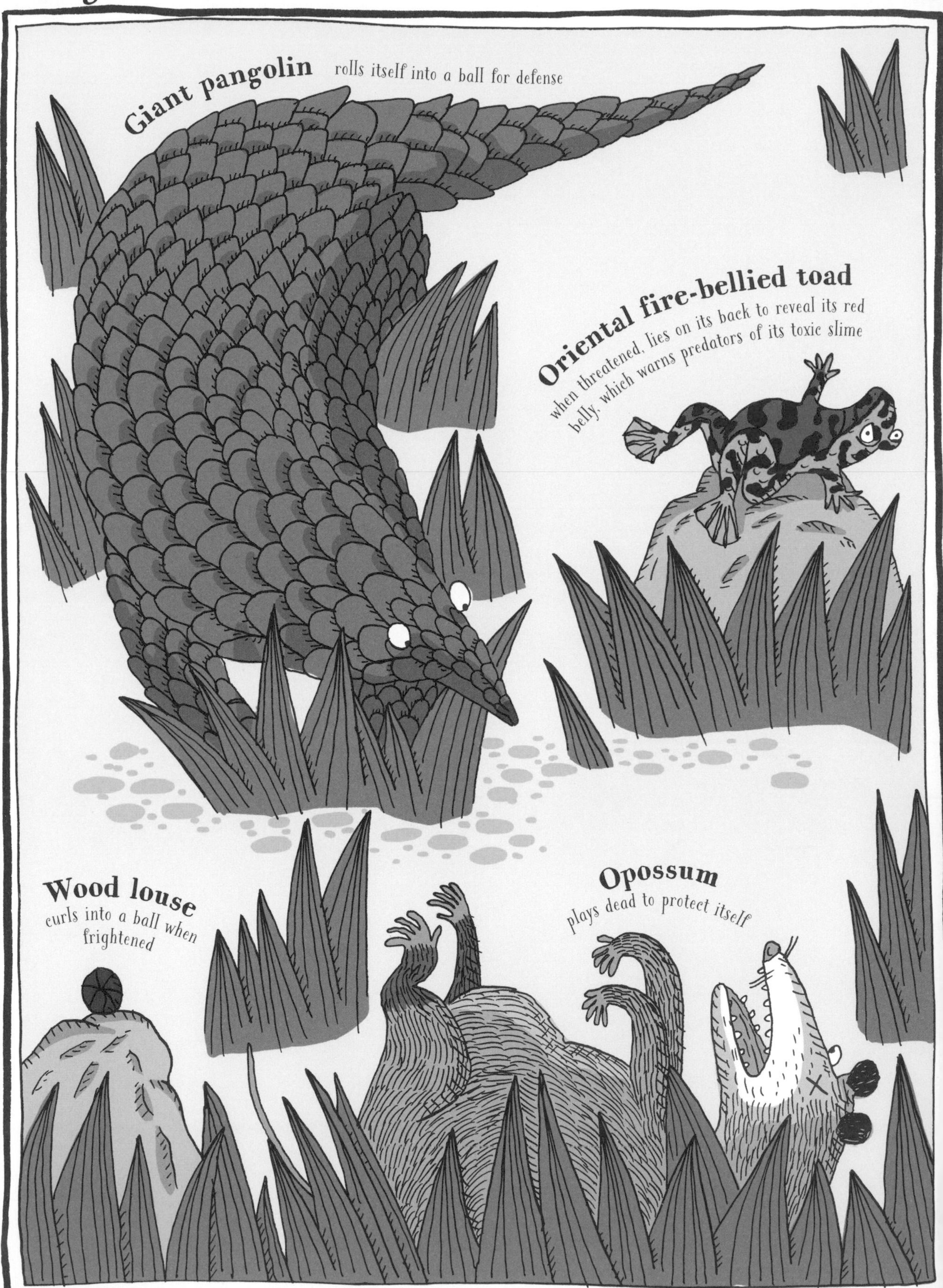
Giant pangolin
rolls itself into a ball for defense
Oriental fire-bellied toad
when threatened, lies on its back to reveal its red belly, which warns predators of its toxic slime
Wood louse
curls into a ball when frightened
Opossum
plays dead to protect itself

Chinese box turtle
hides in shell if a predator approaches
Longhorn cowfish
body is protected by a shell of bony plates
Striped eel catfish
shoal forms a tightly packed ball to confuse attackers
Sea cucumber
squirts out sticky threads to ensnare predators

The homebodies

Wild boar
remains in one territory, leaving only if food runs short

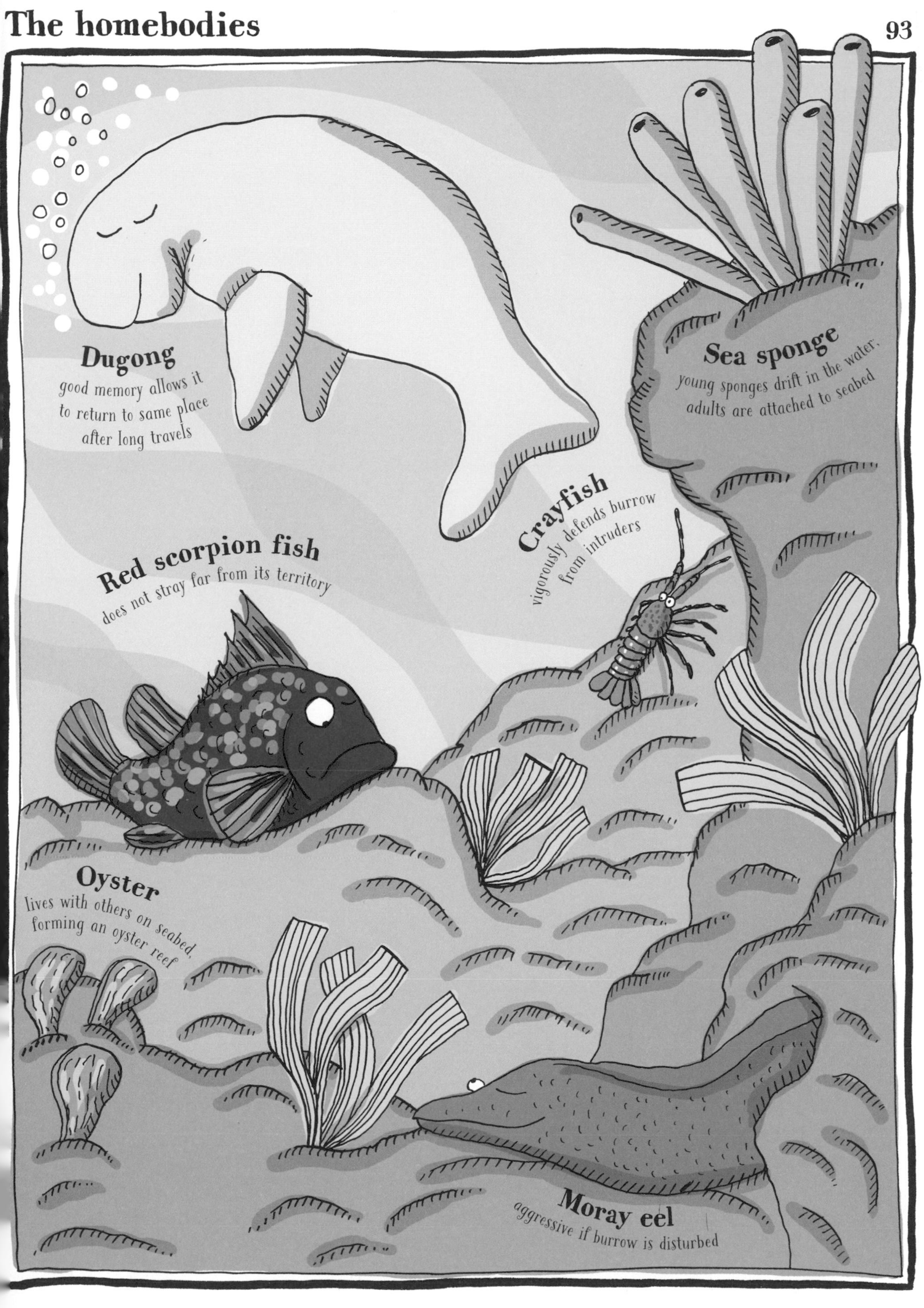
Dugong
good memory allows it to return to same place after long travels
Sea sponge
young sponges drift in the water, adults are attached to seabed
Crayfish
vigorously defends burrow from intruders
Red scorpion fish
does not stray far from its territory
Oyster
lives with others on seabed, forming an oyster reef
Moray eel
aggressive if burrow is disturbed

Magpie
breeding pairs have territory of about 12 acres
Hermann's tortoise
strong homing instinct
Common kingfisher
very territorial; controls a stretch of river

The Lilliputians

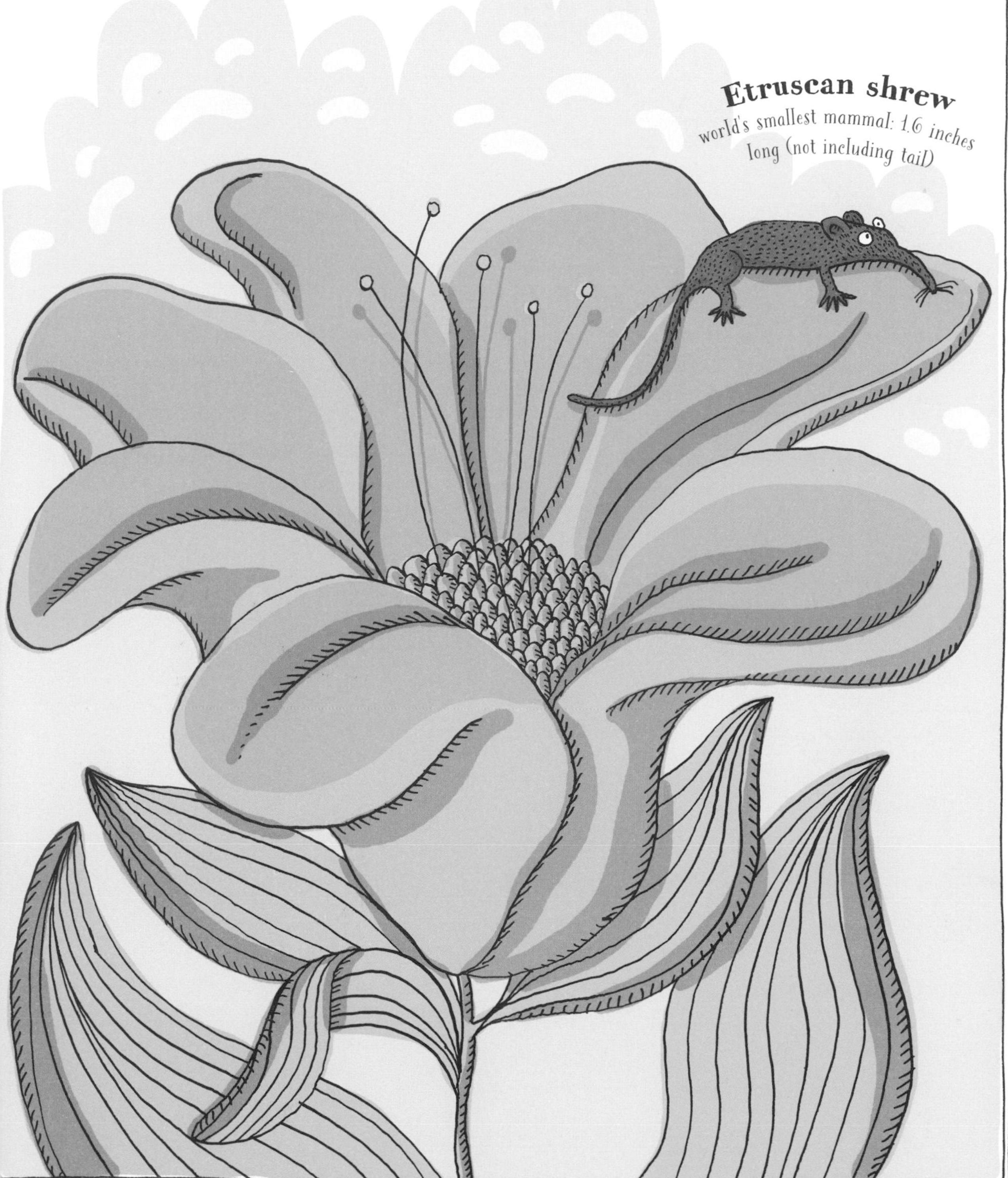

Red panda
22 inches long
(not including tail)
Lesser white-
fronted goose
24 inches long

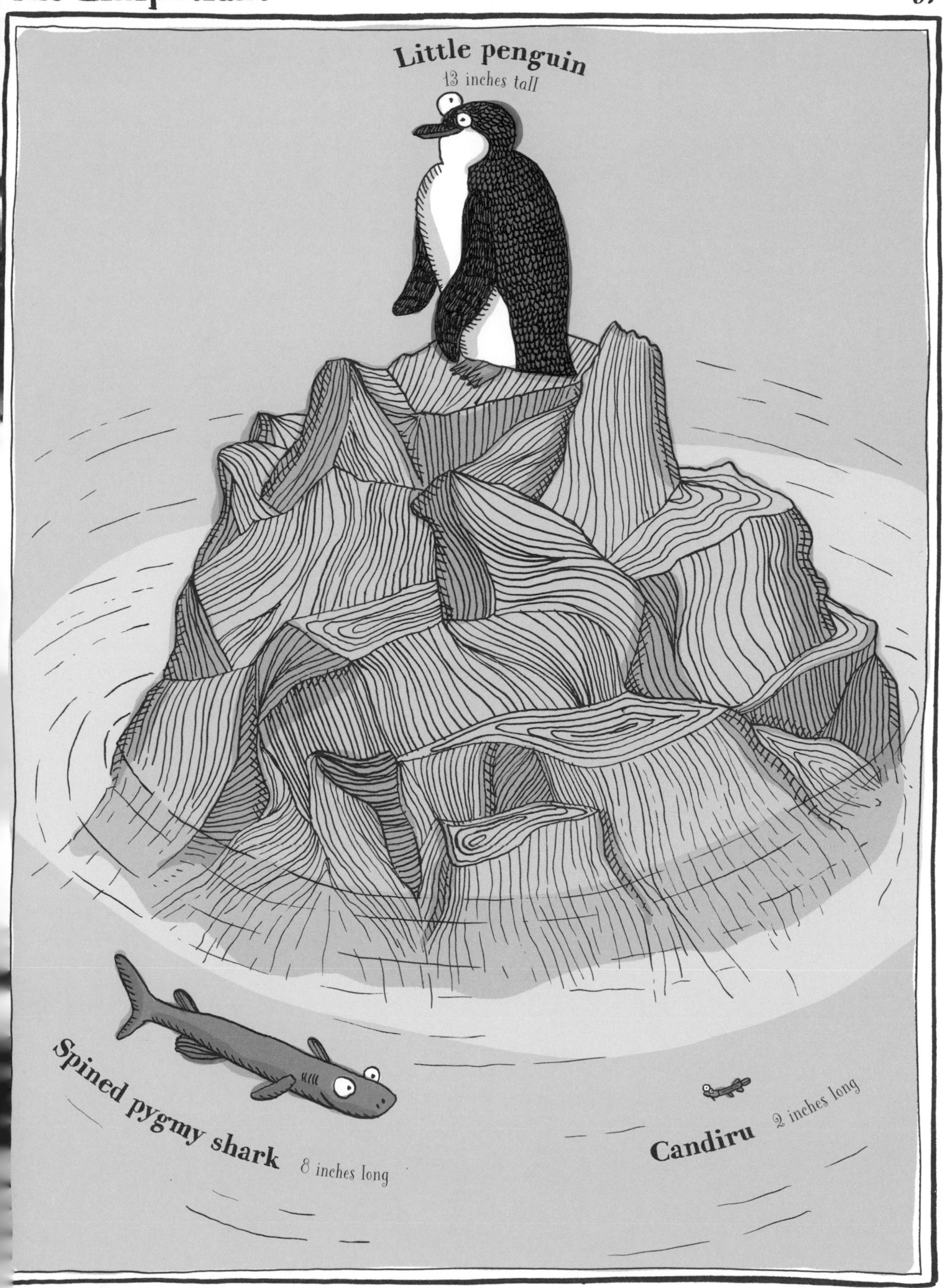
Little penguin
13 inches tall
Spined pygmy shark
8 inches long
Candiru
2 inches long

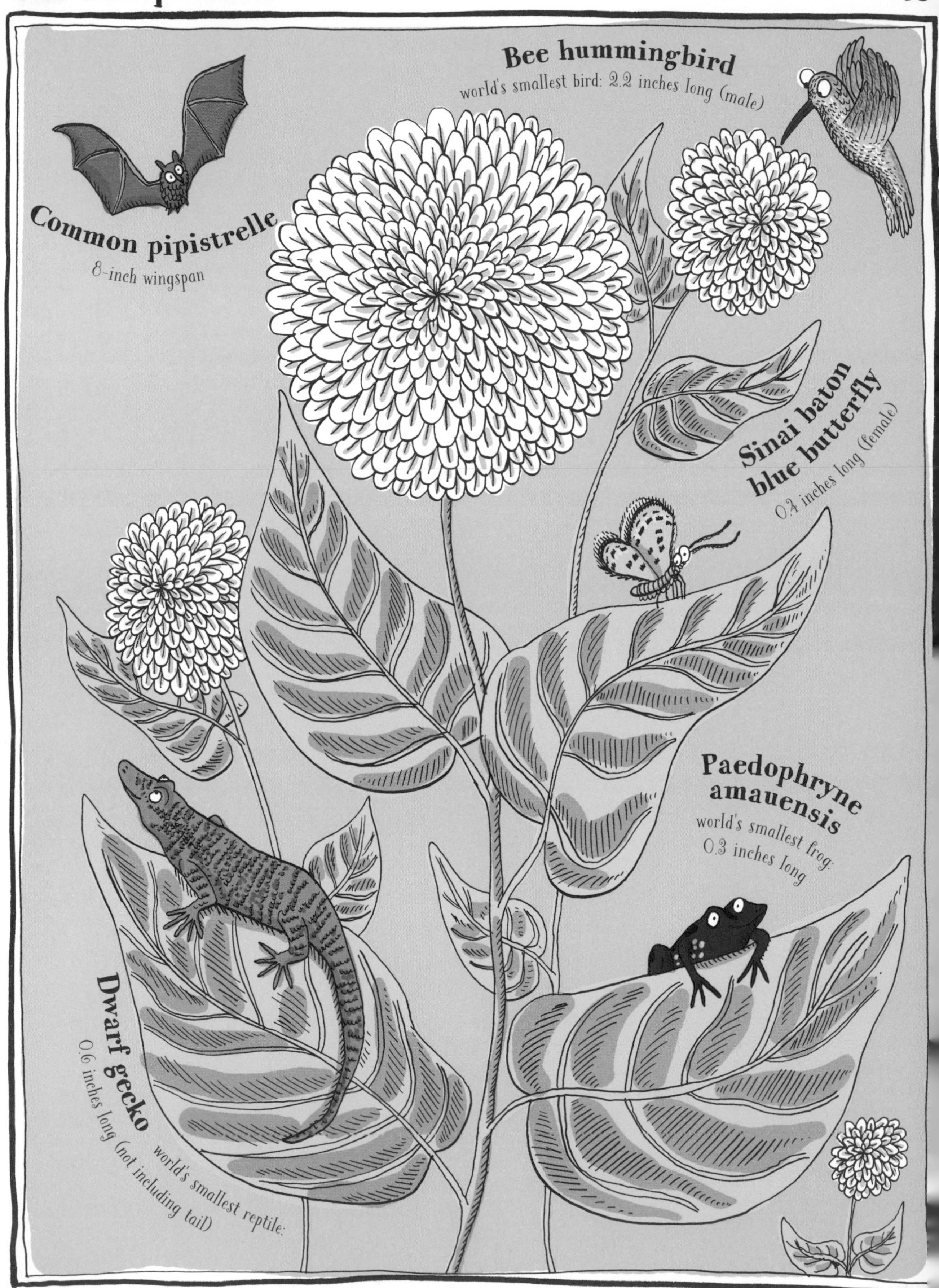
Bee hummingbird
world's smallest bird: 2.2 inches long (male)
Common pipistrelle
8-inch wingspan
Sinai baton blue butterfly
0.4 inches long (female)
Paedophryne amauensis
world's smallest frog: 0.3 inches long
Dwarf gecko
world's smallest reptile: 0.6 inches long (not including tail)

Galápagos sea lion
6.5 feet long
Pygmy hippopotamus
31 inches at shoulder
Pygmy falcon
7.5 inches long
Pony
less than 58 inches at shoulder
Alpaca
35 inches at shoulder

The long-necked

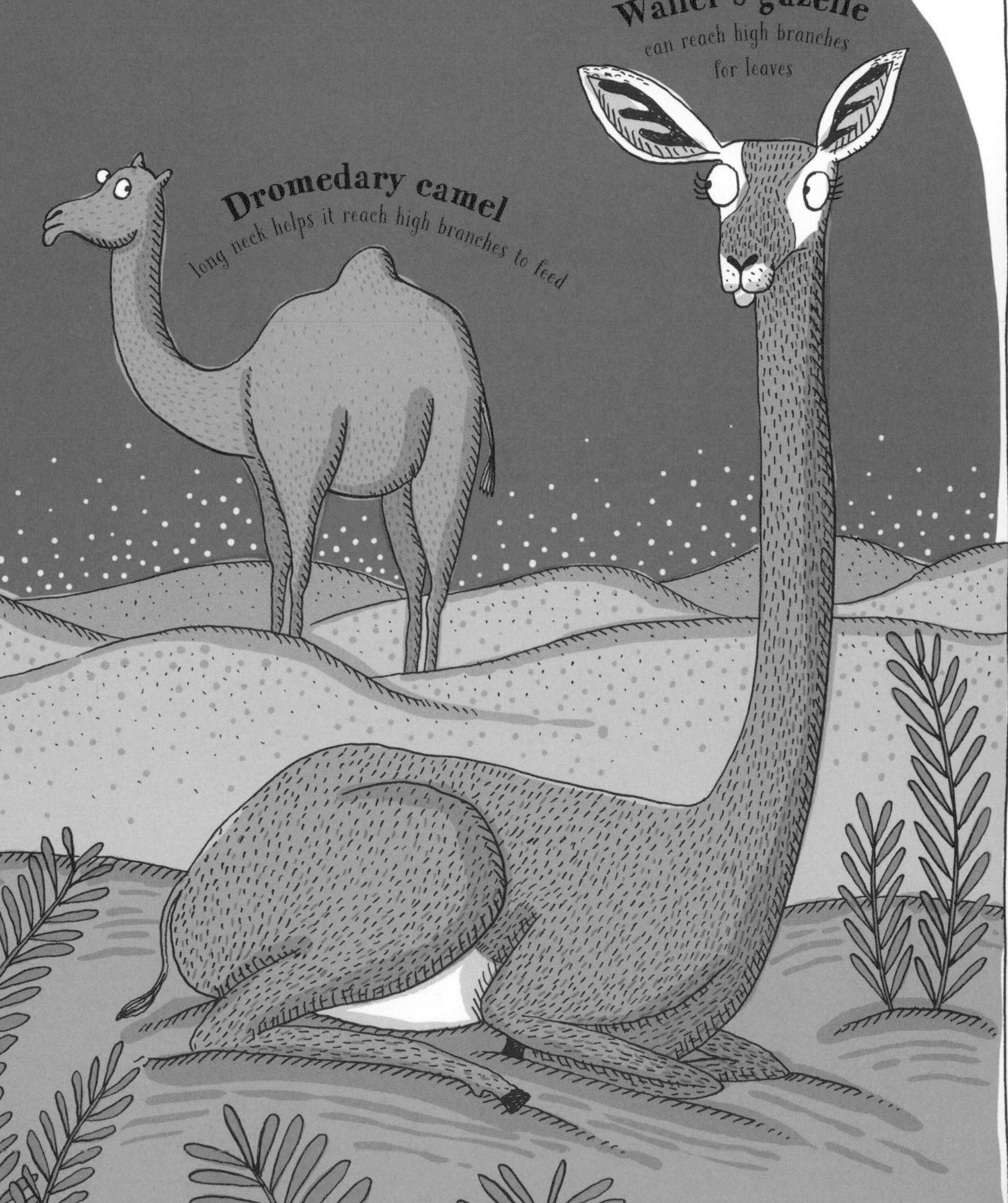

Waller's gazelle
can reach high branches
for leaves
Dromedary camel
long neck helps it reach high branches to feed

California sea lion
long, flexible neck makes it an agile swimmer
Purple heron
extends long neck to catch fish

Mute swan
can't dive, so uses neck to reach food on lakes and riverbeds
Great egret
tucks neck in when flying
Great crested grebe
neck helps reach fish when diving underwater
Eastern long-necked turtle
neck allows it to breathe at surface while body is hidden underwater

Guanaco
skin on neck is extra-thick to protect against puma bites
Greater rhea
can easily scan for danger thanks to long neck
Giraffe weevil (male)
uses neck for fighting other males and building a nest

The long-tongued

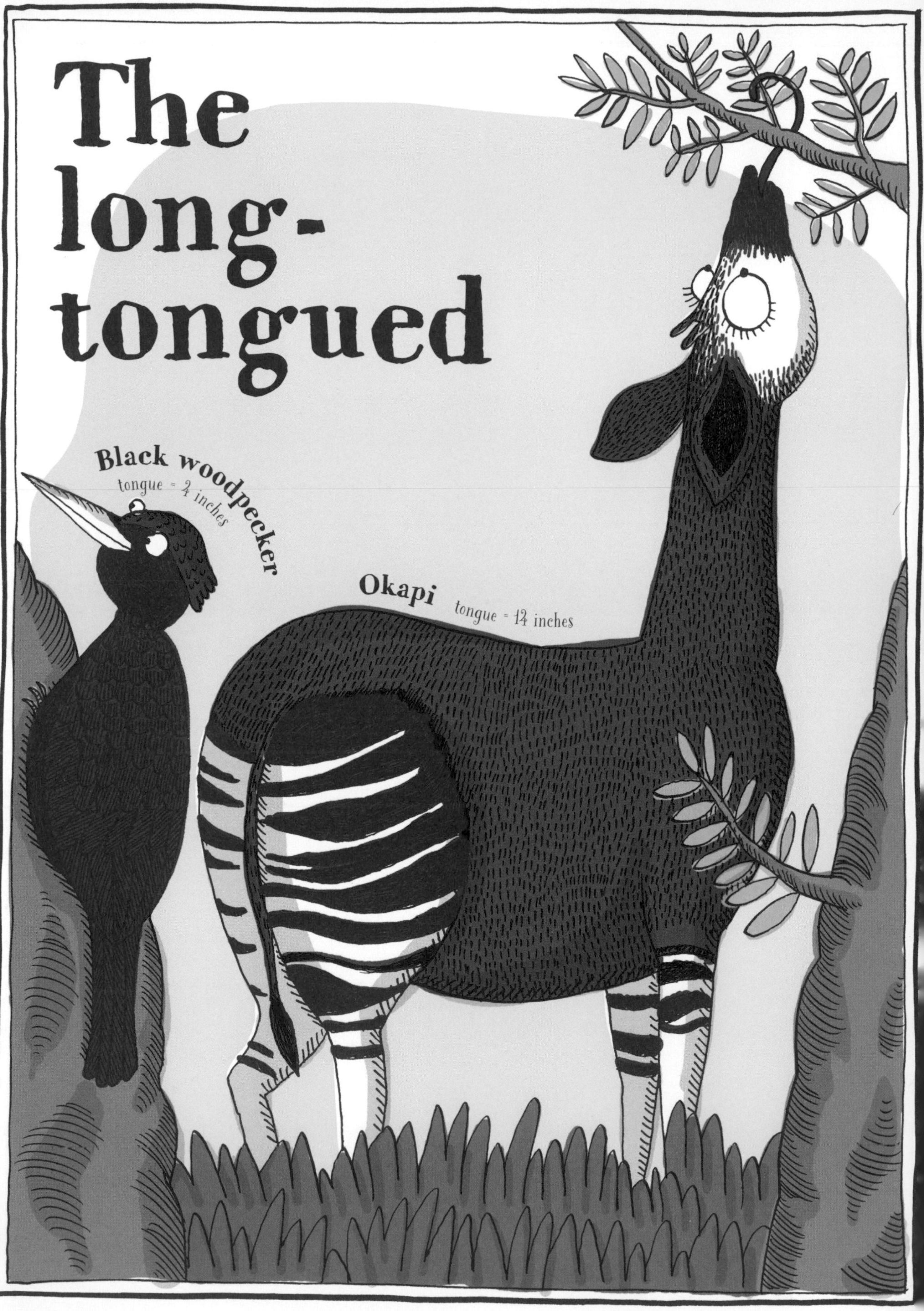

Black woodpecker
tongue = 4 inches

Okapi tongue = 14 inches

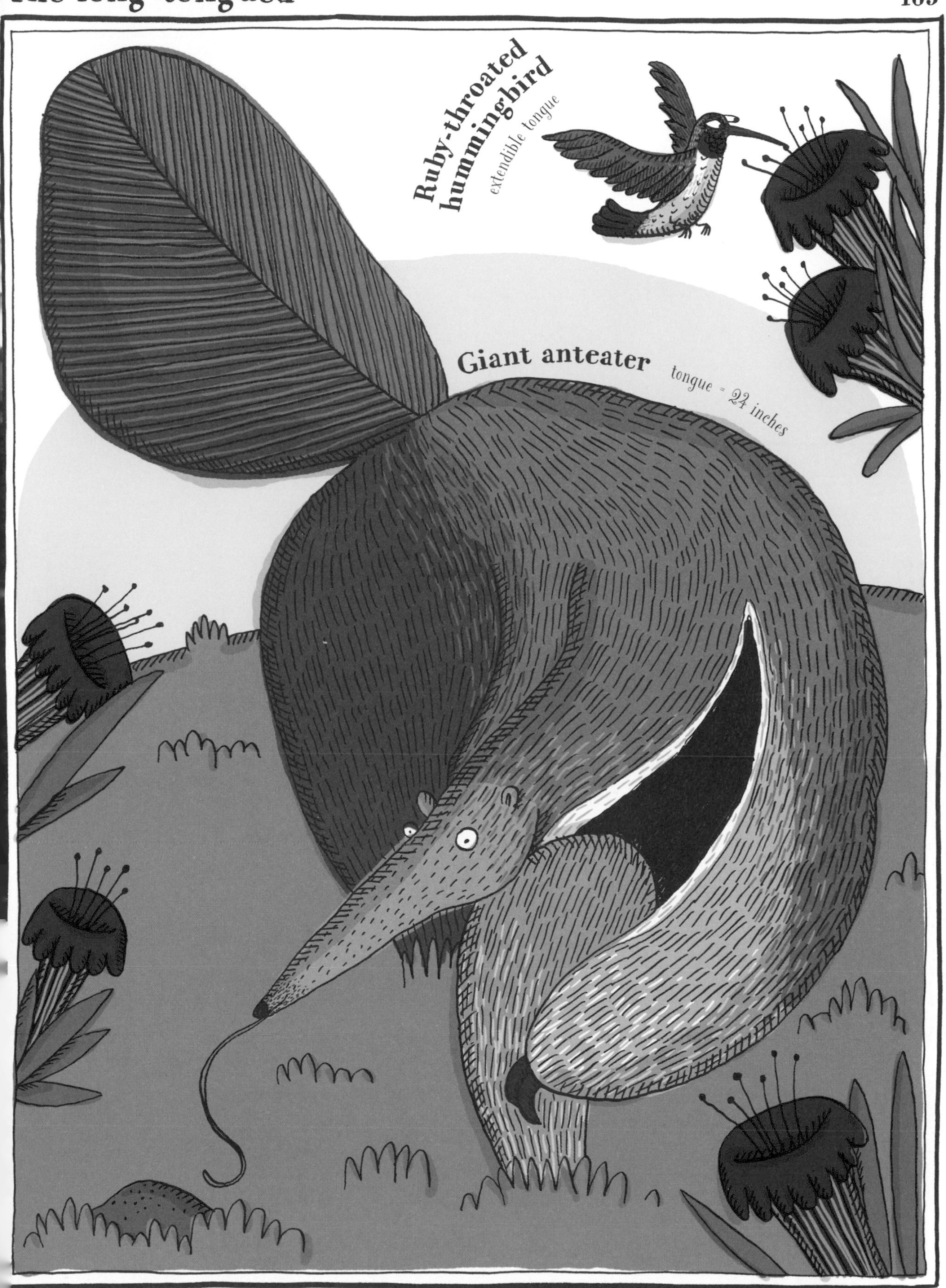
Ruby-throated hummingbird
extendible tongue
Giant anteater
tongue = 24 inches

Giraffe
tongue = 20 inches
Chameleon
tongue is longer than body
Sun bear
tongue = 10 inches
Honey possum
brush-tipped tongue
collects pollen

The masters of camouflage

Weedy sea dragon
Stonefish
Sole
Undulate ray

Elegant crested tinamou
Common snipe
Diamond rattlesnake
Common spadefoot toad
Flower crab spider

Sycamore moth
Leaf-tailed gecko
Common chameleon
Stick insect
Satanic leaf-tailed gecko

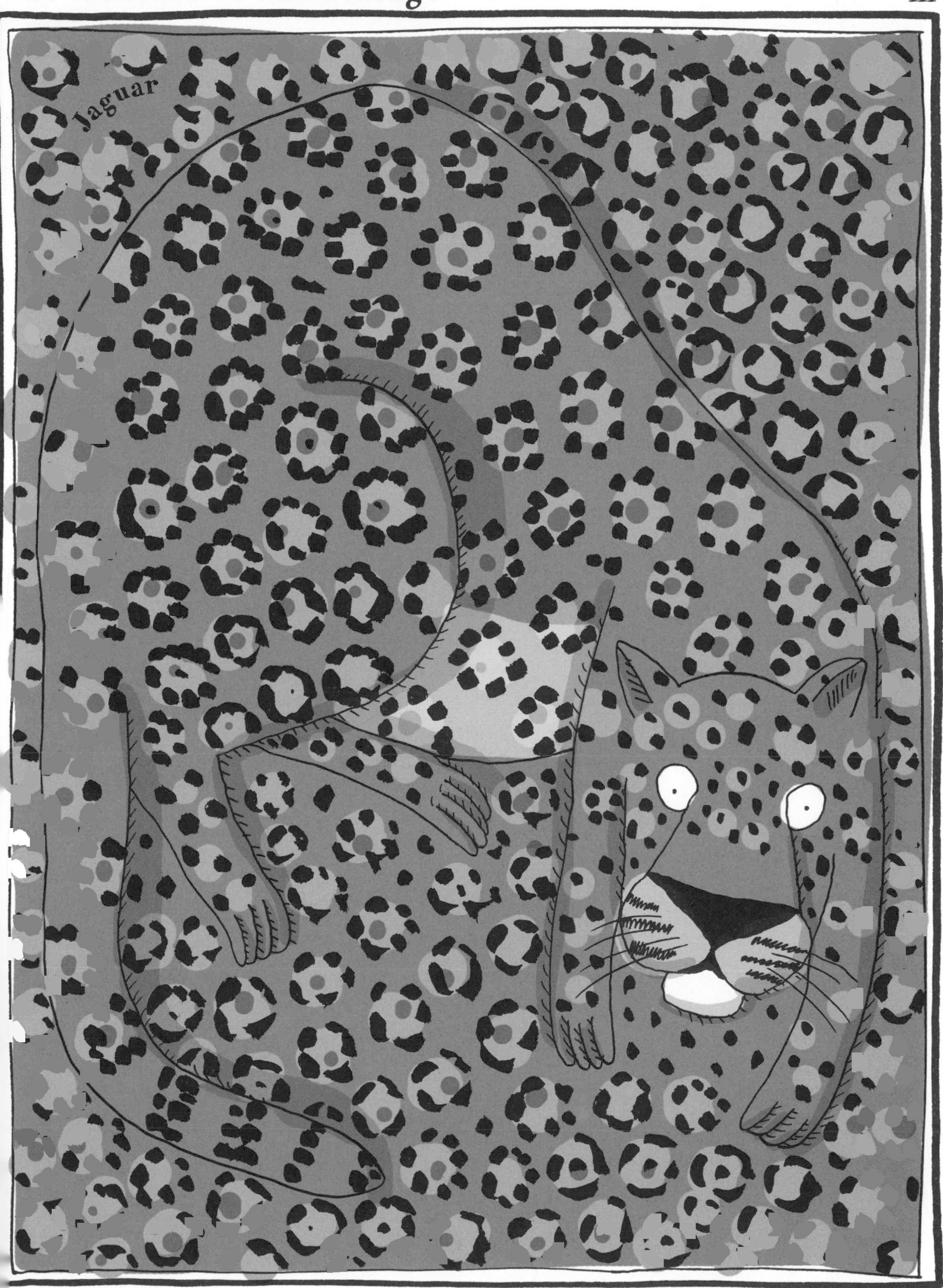
Jaguar

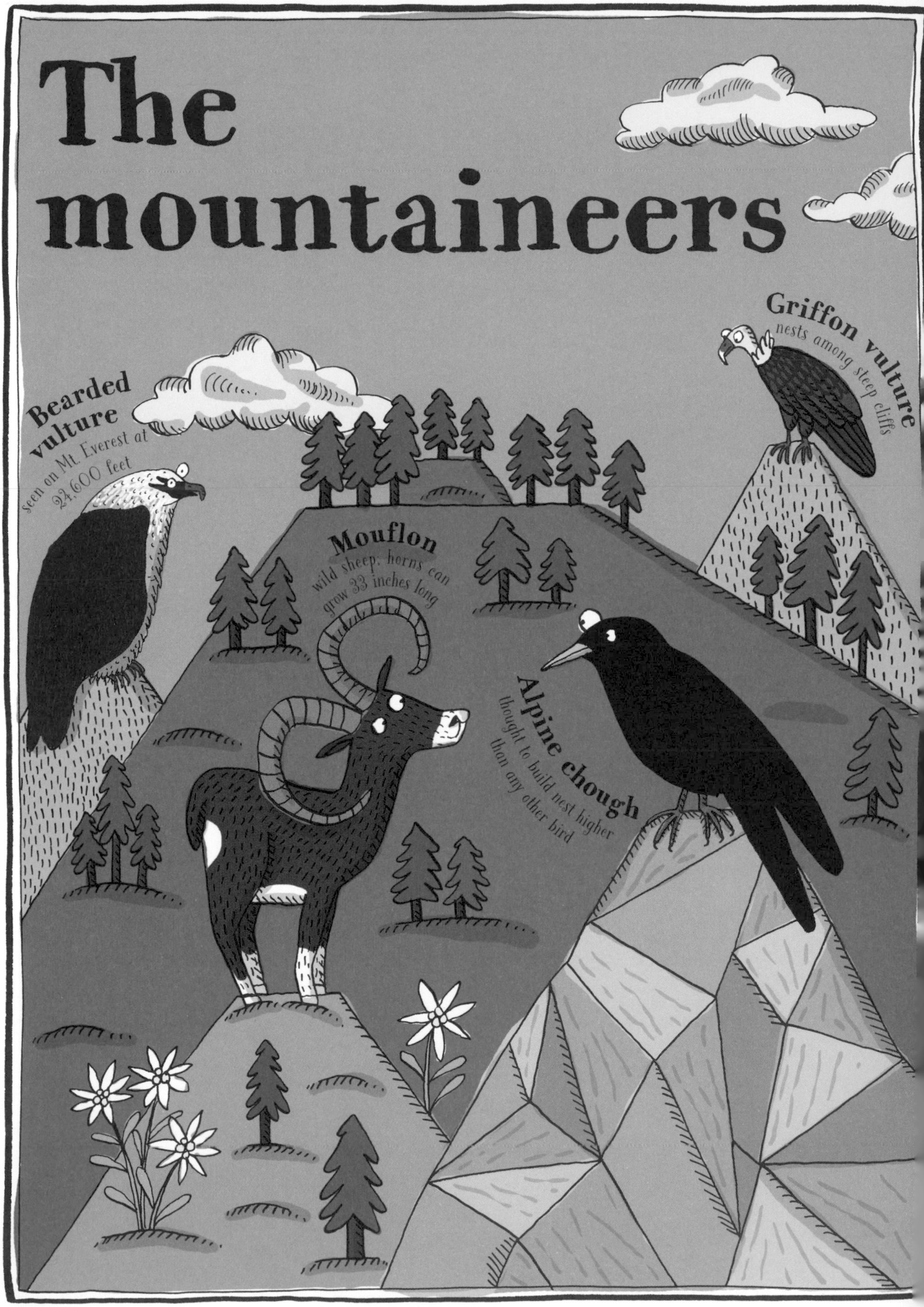

The mountaineers

Bearded vulture
seen on Mt. Everest at 24,600 feet

Mouflon
wild sheep; horns can grow 33 inches long

Griffon vulture
nests among steep cliffs

Alpine chough
thought to build nest higher than any other bird

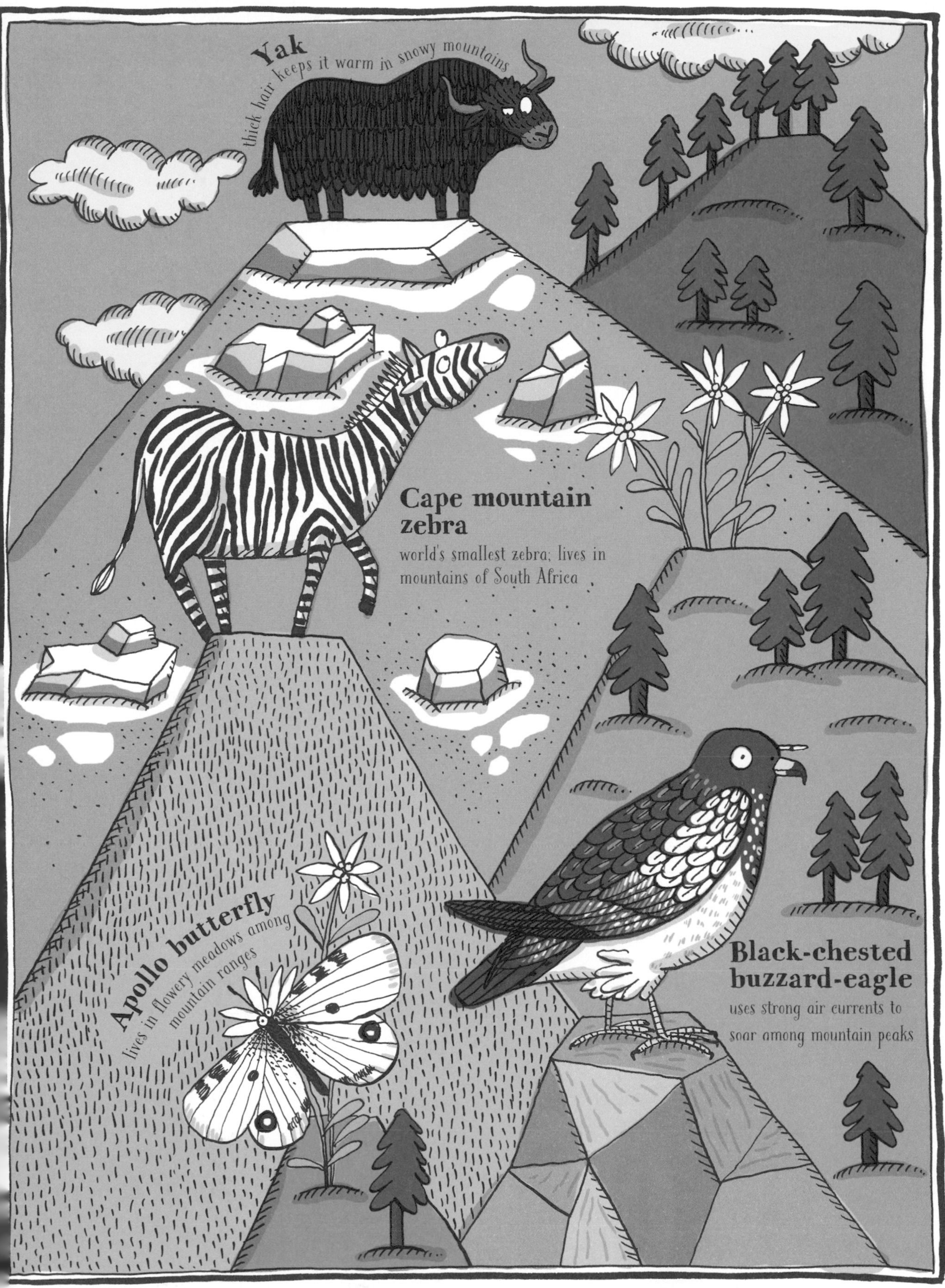
Yak
thick hair keeps it warm in snowy mountains
Cape mountain zebra
world's smallest zebra; lives in mountains of South Africa
Apollo butterfly
lives in flowery meadows among mountain ranges
Black-chested buzzard-eagle
uses strong air currents to soar among mountain peaks

Andean condor
huge 10-foot wingspan; glides on air currents
Rock ptarmigan
molts to change color so blends in as seasons turn
Marmot
hibernates in group burrow during freezing winter

Chamois
can run at 30 mph
on uneven ground
Lake trout
lives in cold lakes, often
200 feet deep
Alpine newt (male)
lives in water during mating season;
male's color changes to attract a mate

The munch-it-uppers

Tiger hunts in darkness with night vision six times better than humans'

Barracuda dagger-like teeth
Orca tips up ice floes to knock seals and penguins into water to eat
Swordfish uses swordlike bill to slash at prey

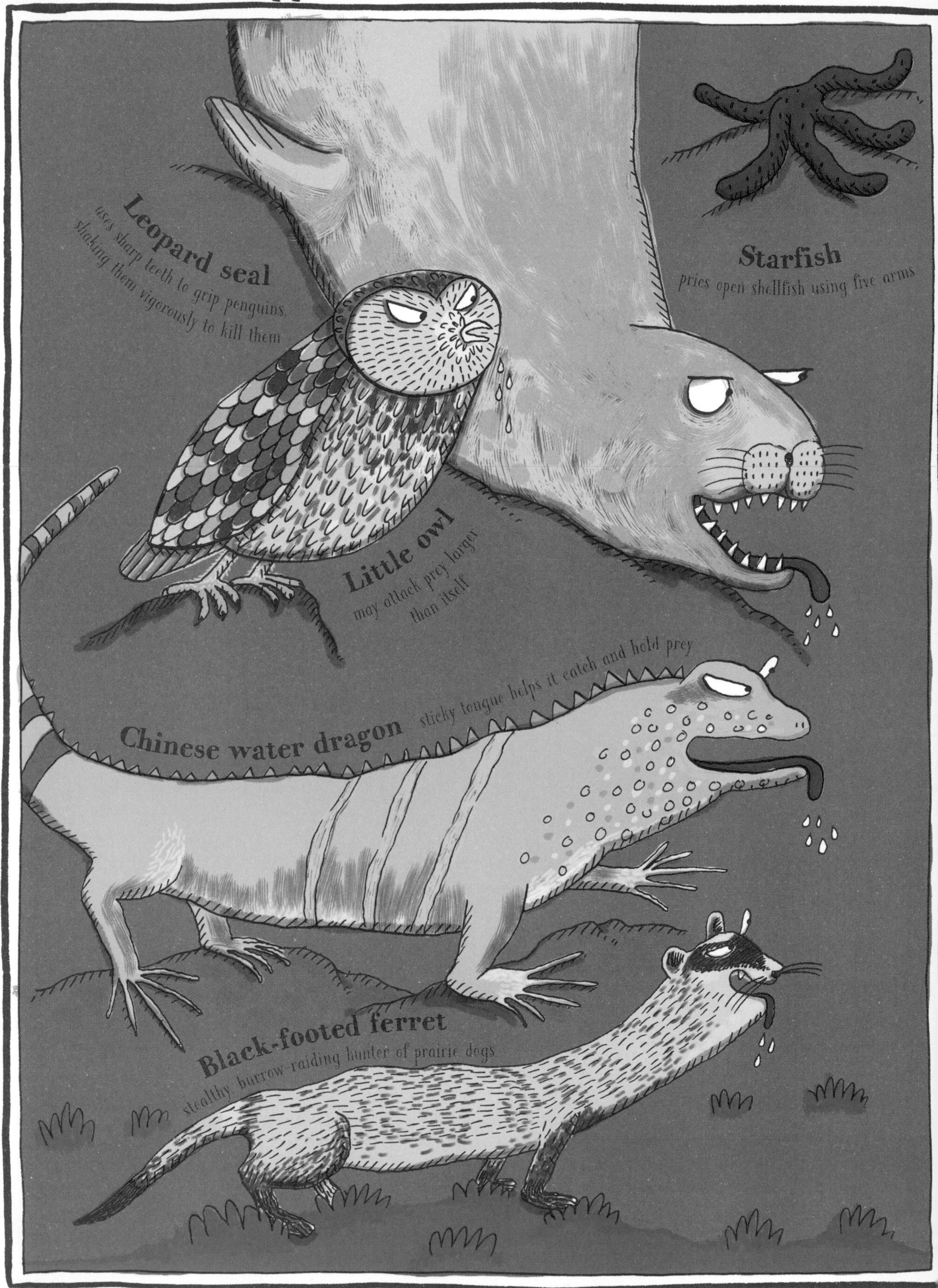
Leopard seal
uses sharp teeth to grip penguins, shaking them vigorously to kill them
Starfish
pries open shellfish using five arms
Little owl
may attack prey larger than itself
Chinese water dragon
sticky tongue helps it catch and hold prey
Black-footed ferret
stealthy, burrow-raiding hunter of prairie dogs

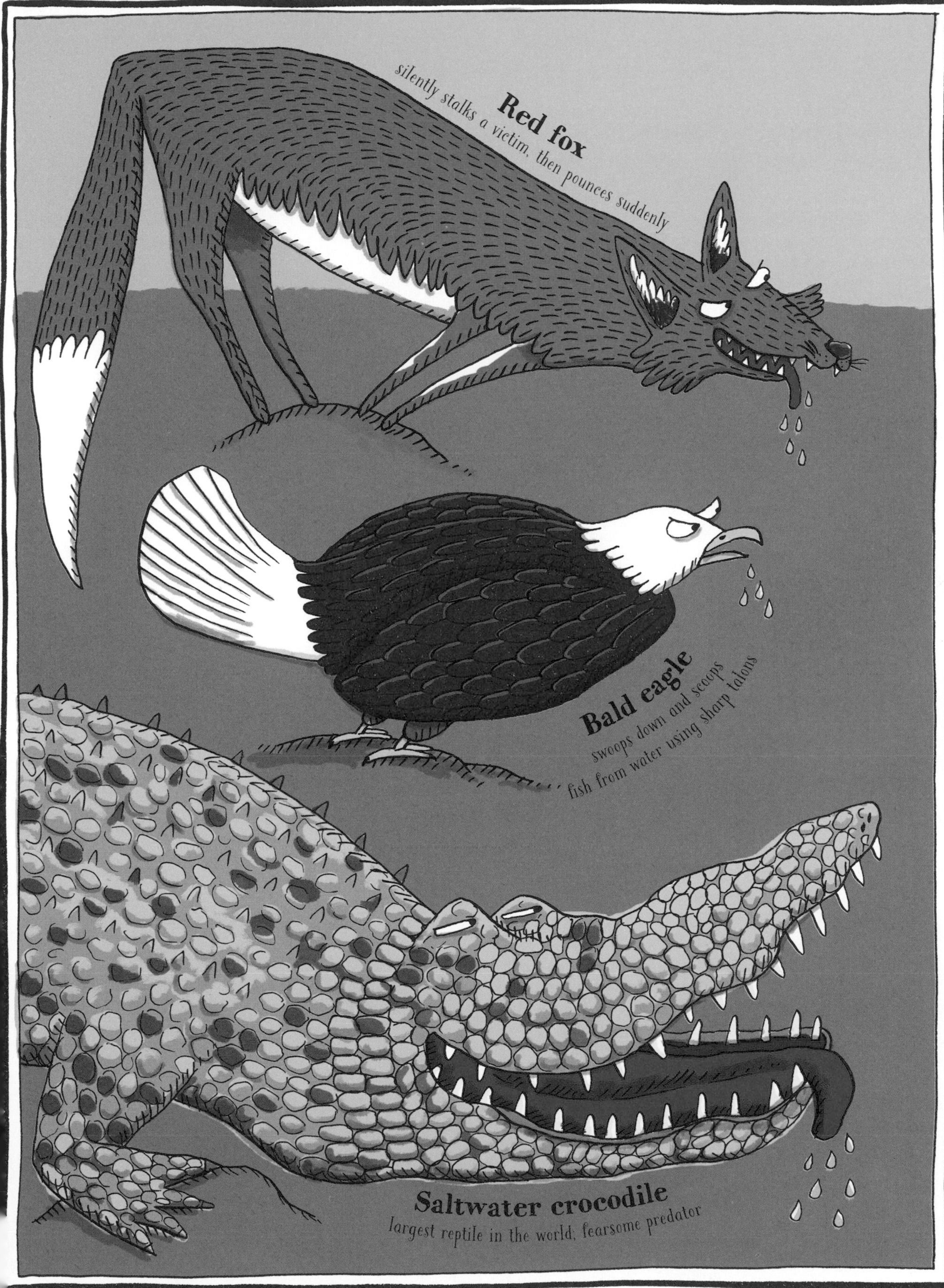
Red fox
silently stalks a victim, then pounces suddenly
Bald eagle
swoops down and scoops fish from water using sharp talons
Saltwater crocodile
largest reptile in the world; fearsome predator

Montagu's harrier
drops from sky to catch prey by surprise
Muskellunge
eats prey headfirst, sometimes in a single massive gulp

The mythical
Pegasus
Yeti
Dahu
mountain goat with legs on one side shorter than other side

Roc
Cerberus
Unicorn

Dragon
Snouter
small mammal that uses nose
for everything, including jumping
and fishing

Griffin
Lernaean Hydra
Baku
eater of nightmares

The night owls

Eurasian eagle-owl
night vision, powerful hearing, and silent flight make it a deadly predator

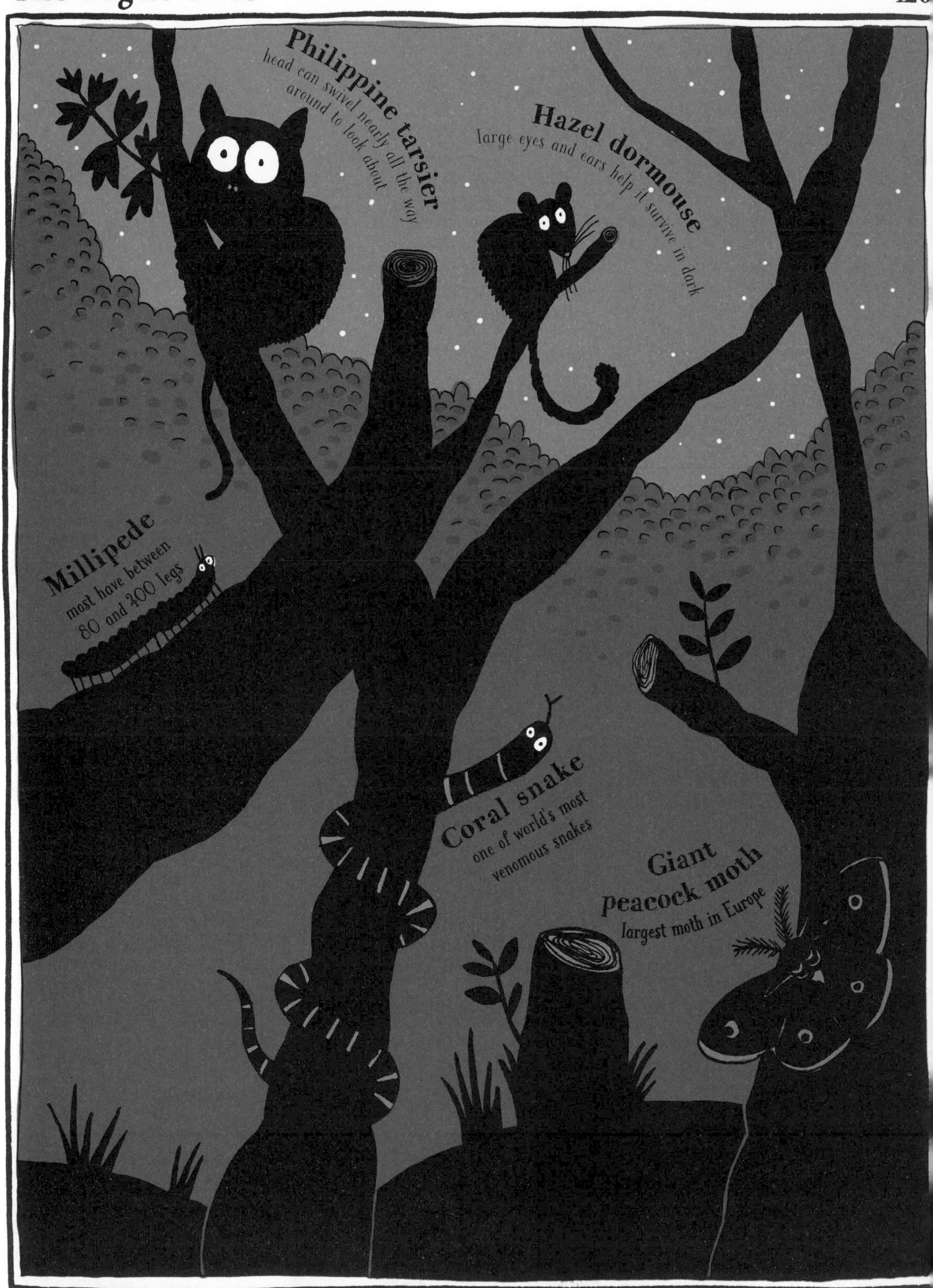
Philippine tarsier
head can swivel nearly all the way around to look about
Hazel dormouse
large eyes and ears help it survive in dark
Millipede
most have between 80 and 400 legs
Coral snake
one of world's most venomous snakes
Giant peacock moth
largest moth in Europe

Sloth
world's slowest mammal; spends most of life hanging upside down
Badger
strong sense of smell helps it find food in dark
Crocodile gecko

European conger eel
Asian tree toad
toes have sticky discs that help it climb trees
Red-eyed tree frog
sleeps during day with red eyes closed, to hide from hunters

Brazilian tapir
hides in water to avoid attackers, using snout as a snorkel
Stone loach
Squirrelfish
Kiwi
shy, flightless bird, lives only in New Zealand
Spanish moon moth

Barn owl
excellent hearing helps it find prey even in pitch-dark; one ear
is slightly higher than other, helping owl pinpoint sounds

The pack animals

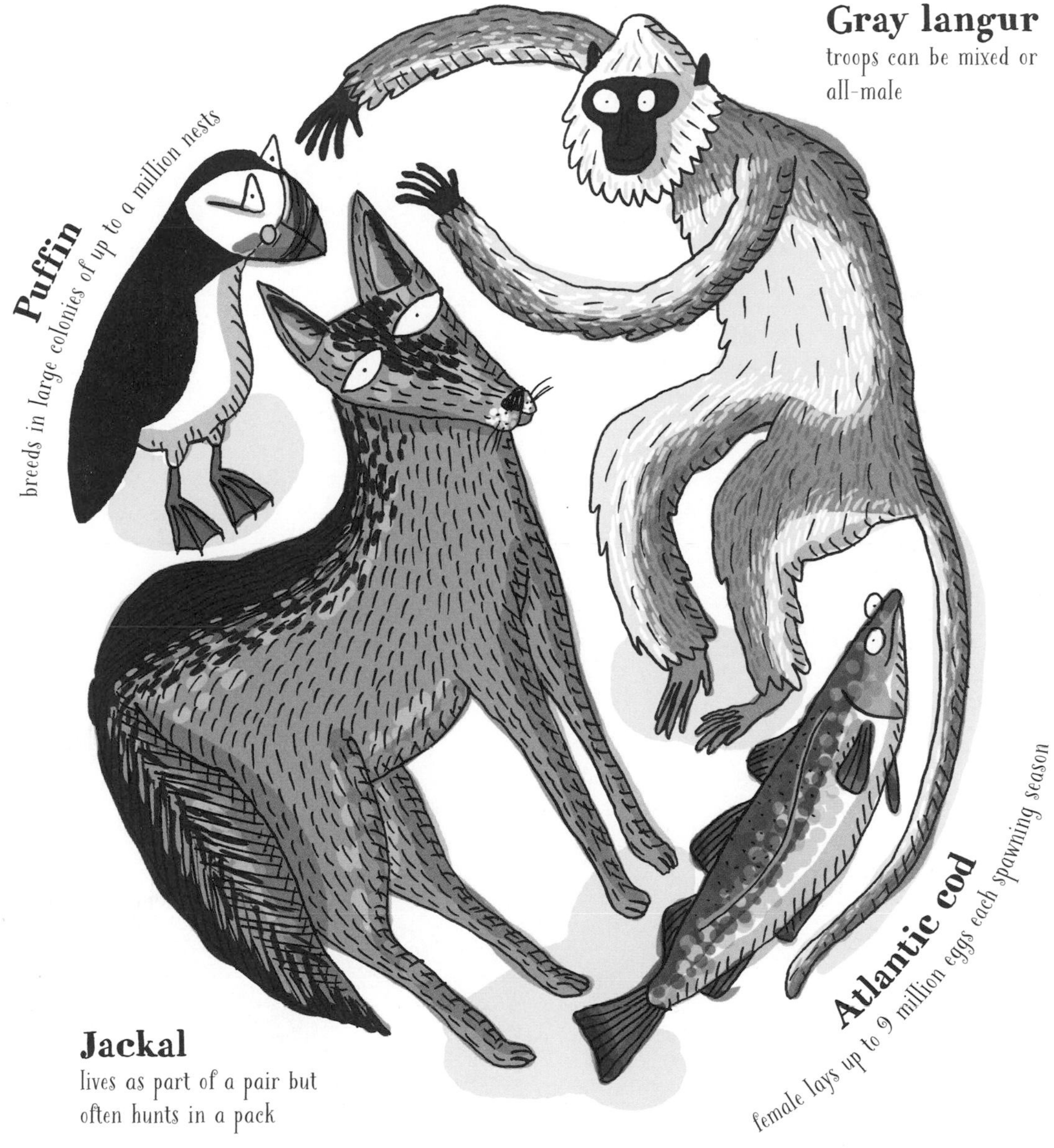

Gray langur
troops can be mixed or all-male
Puffin
breeds in large colonies of up to a million nests
Jackal
lives as part of a pair but often hunts in a pack
Atlantic cod
female lays up to 9 million eggs each spawning season

The pack animals

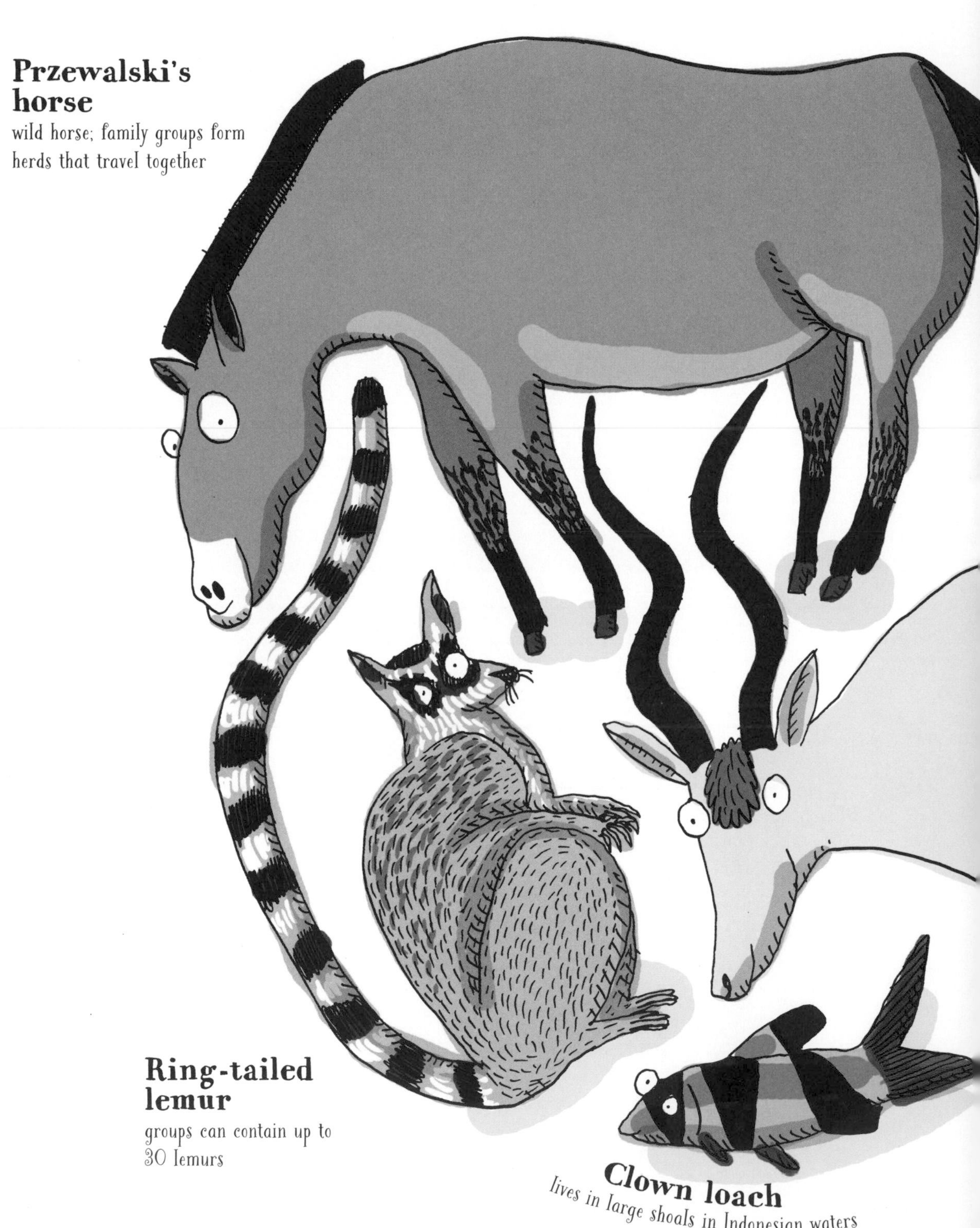

Przewalski's horse
wild horse; family groups form herds that travel together
Ring-tailed lemur
groups can contain up to 30 lemurs
Clown loach
lives in large shoals in Indonesian waters

Hippopotamus
groups, called pods, can contain 100 hippos
European honeybee
lives in a hive of up to 80,000
Addax
lives in a herd of up to 20
Bearded dragon
gathers in groups to feed or sunbathe

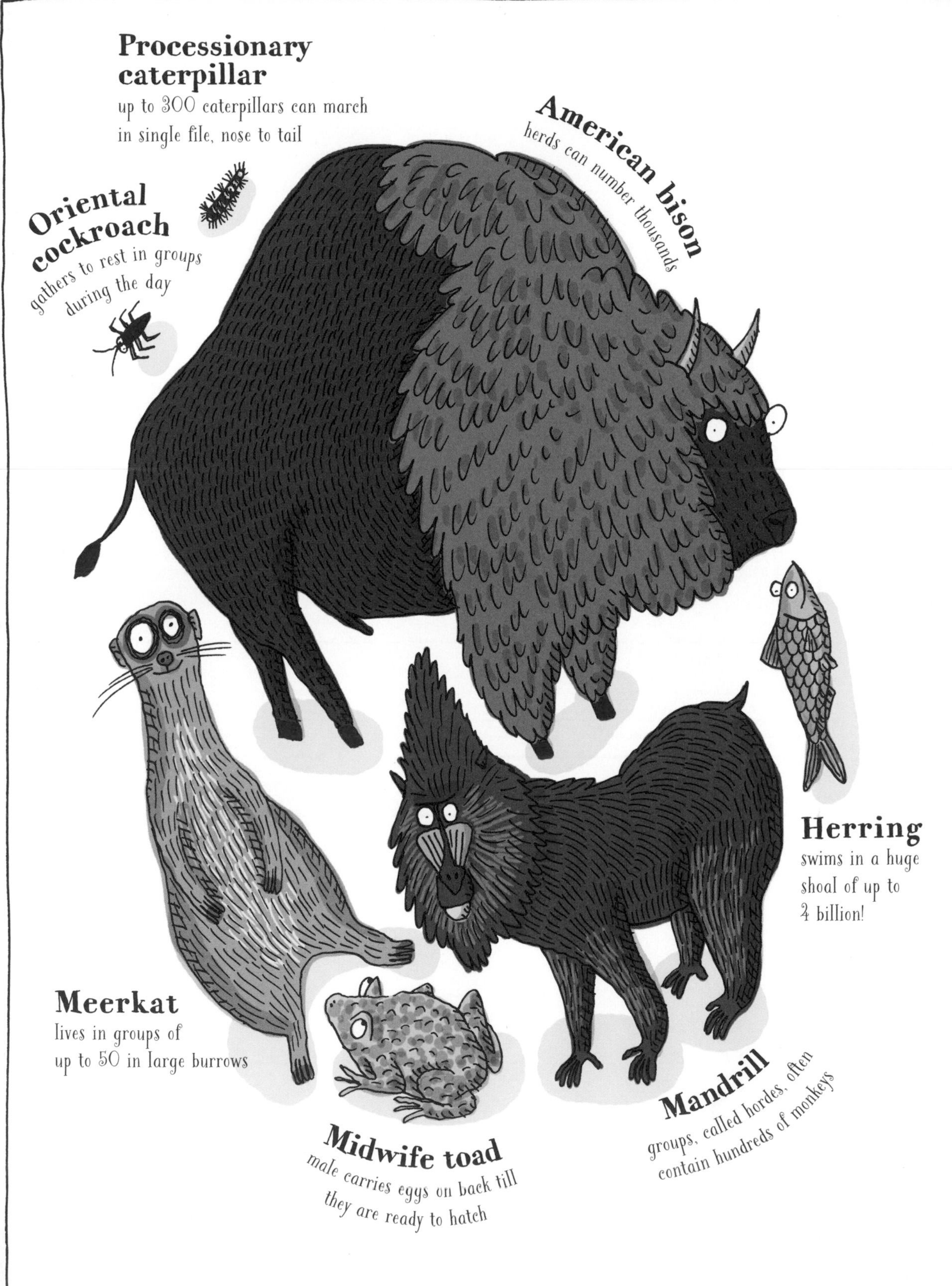
Processionary caterpillar
up to 300 caterpillars can march in single file, nose to tail
American bison
herds can number thousands
Oriental cockroach
gathers to rest in groups during the day
Herring
swims in a huge shoal of up to 4 billion!
Meerkat
lives in groups of up to 50 in large burrows
Mandrill
groups, called hordes, often contain hundreds of monkeys
Midwife toad
male carries eggs on back till they are ready to hatch

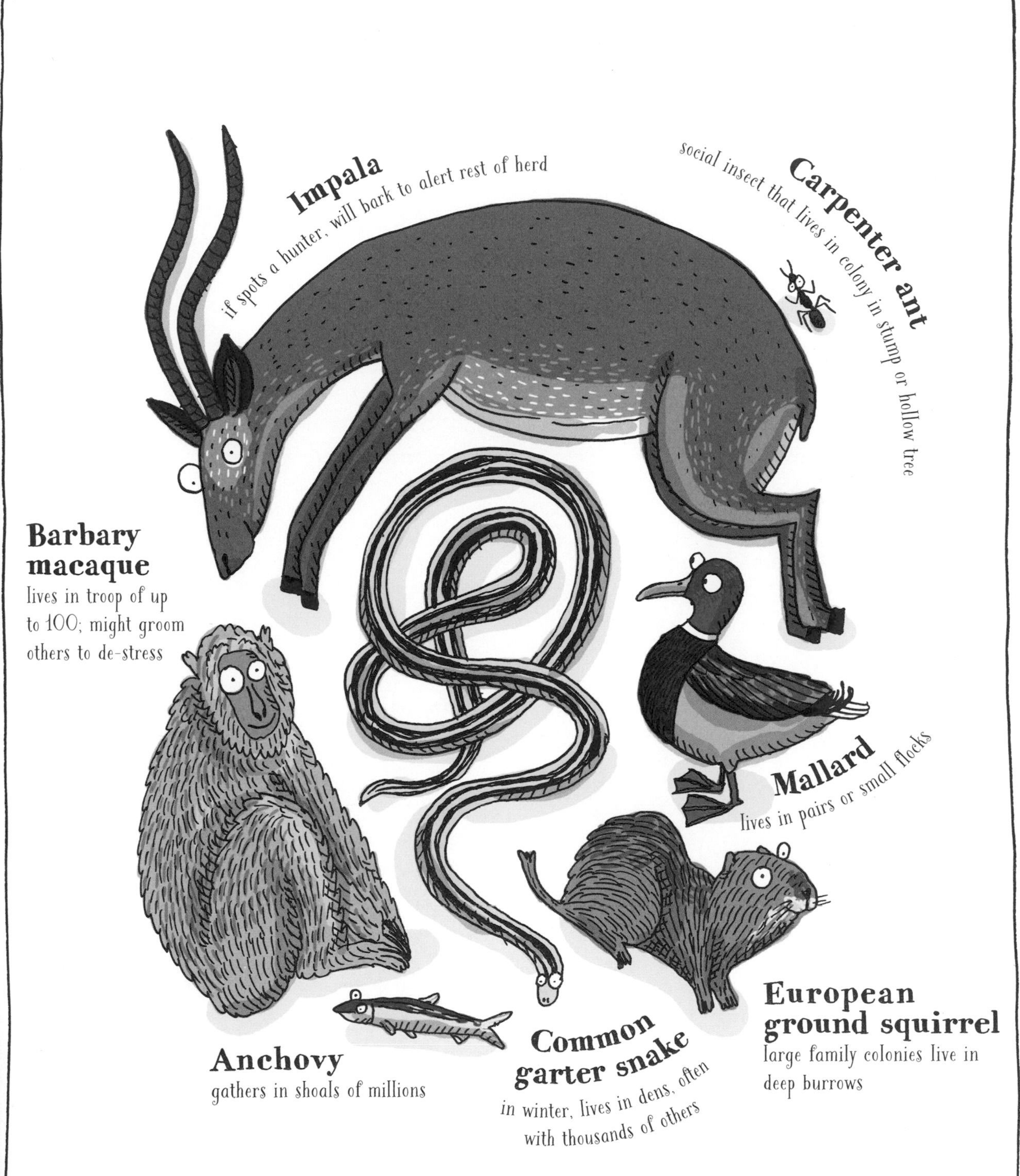
Impala
if spots a hunter, will bark to alert rest of herd
Carpenter ant
social insect that lives in colony in stump or hollow tree
Barbary macaque
lives in troop of up to 100; might groom others to de-stress
Mallard
lives in pairs or small flocks
European ground squirrel
large family colonies live in deep burrows
Anchovy
gathers in shoals of millions
Common garter snake
in winter, lives in dens, often with thousands of others

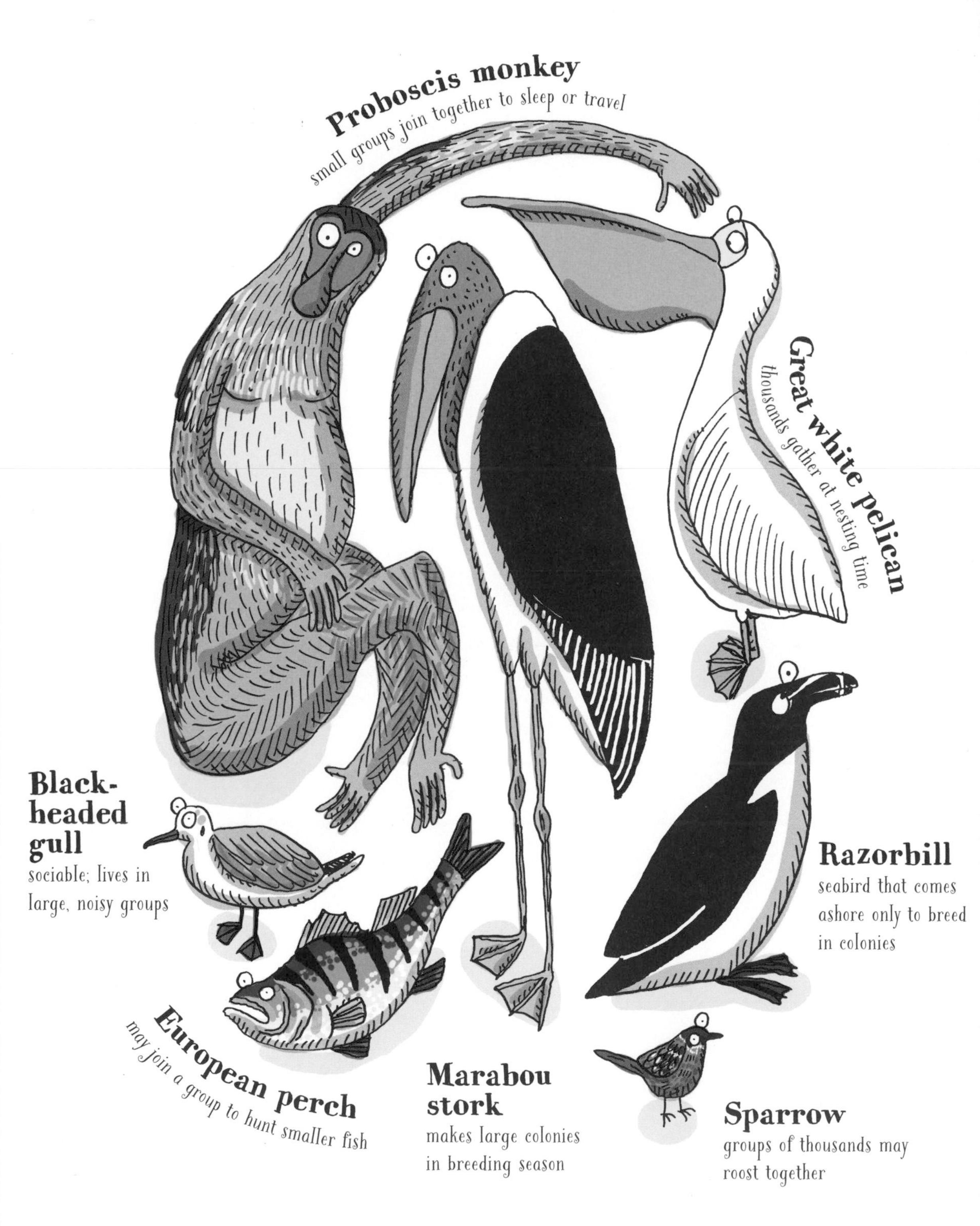
Proboscis monkey
small groups join together to sleep or travel
Great white pelican
thousands gather at nesting time
Black-headed gull
sociable; lives in large, noisy groups
Razorbill
seabird that comes ashore only to breed in colonies
European perch
may join a group to hunt smaller fish
Marabou stork
makes large colonies in breeding season
Sparrow
groups of thousands may roost together

The poisonous

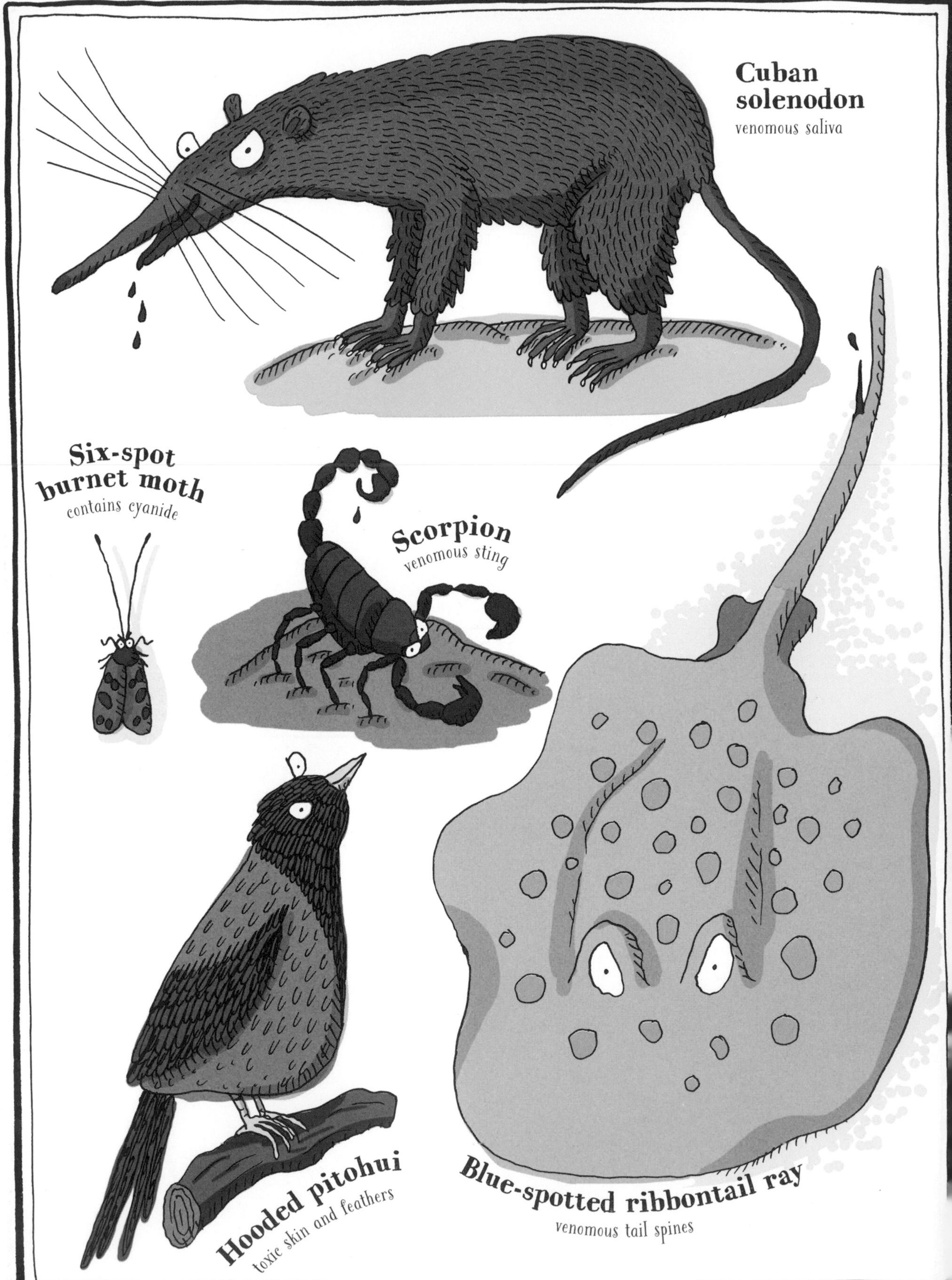
Cuban solenodon
venomous saliva
Six-spot burnet moth
contains cyanide
Scorpion
venomous sting
Hooded pitohui
toxic skin and feathers
Blue-spotted ribbontail ray
venomous tail spines

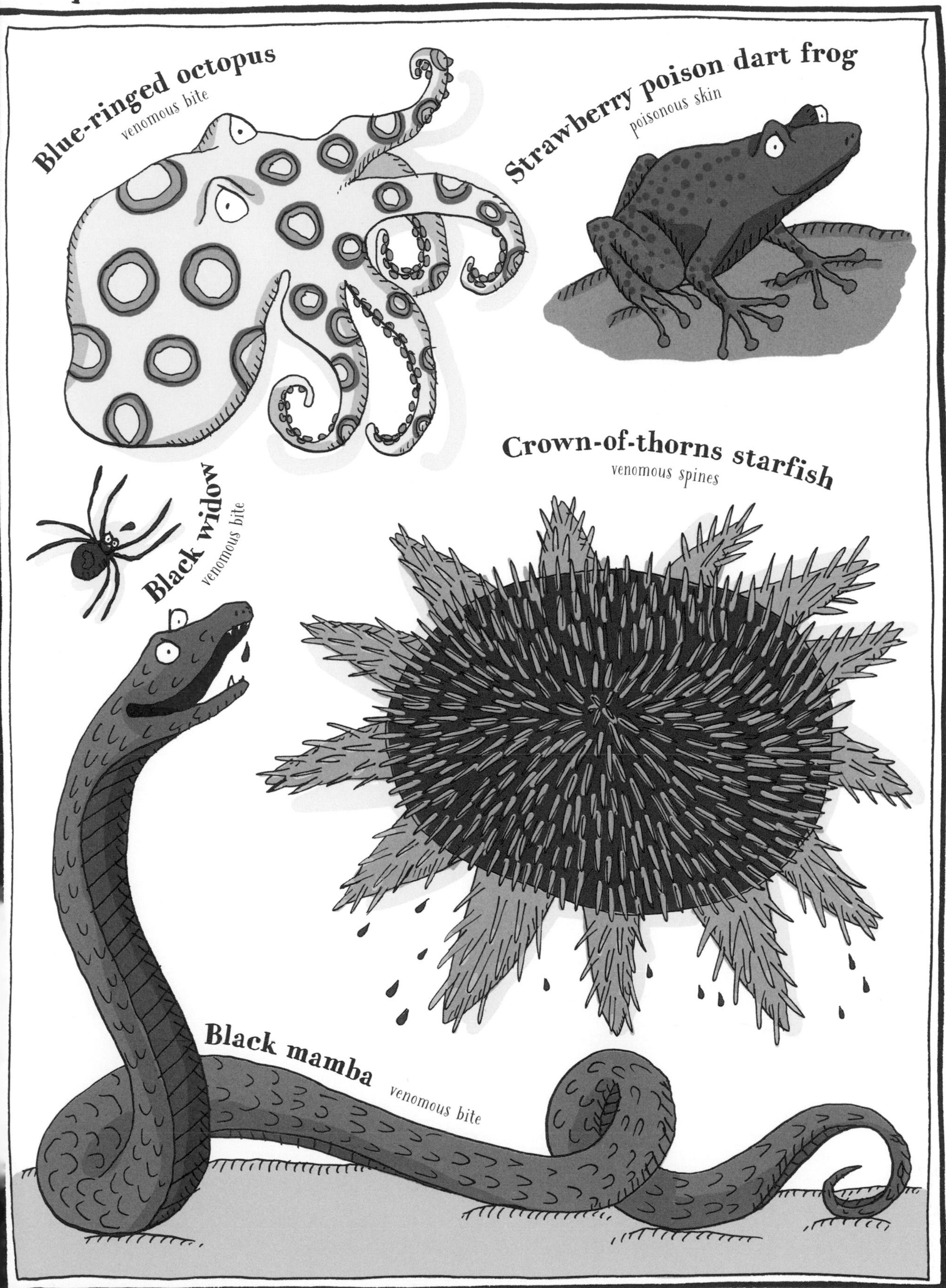
Blue-ringed octopus
venomous bite
Strawberry poison dart frog
poisonous skin
Crown-of-thorns starfish
venomous spines
Black widow
venomous bite
Black mamba
venomous bite

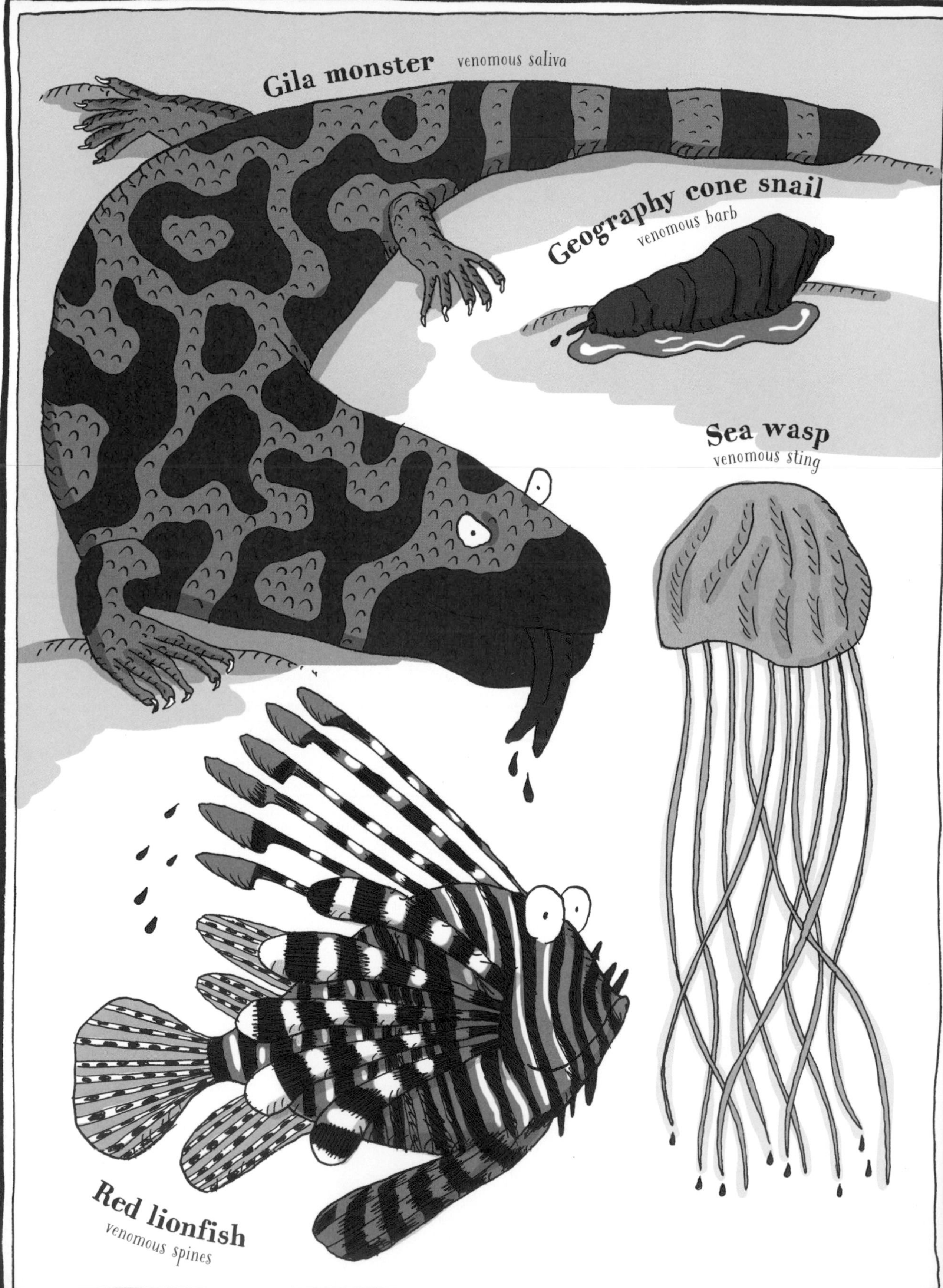
Gila monster
venomous saliva
Geography cone snail
venomous barb
Sea wasp
venomous sting
Red lionfish
venomous spines

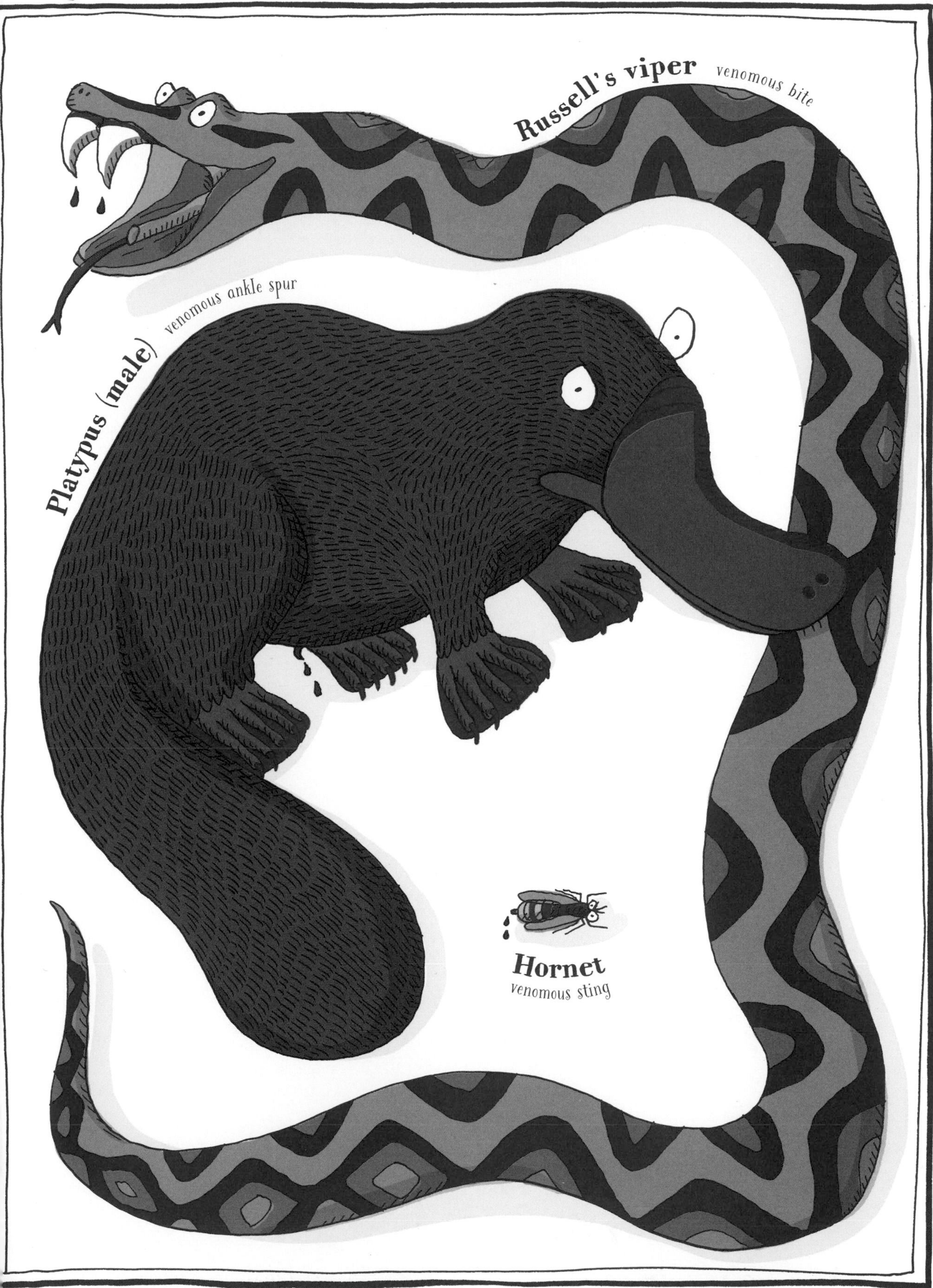
Russell's viper
venomous bite
Platypus (male)
venomous ankle spur
Hornet
venomous sting

The pretty-in-pinks

Earthworm
Elephant hawk moth

Greater flamingo
Roseate spoonbill
Amazon river dolphin

The prickly ones

Spiny anteater
spiky body; some even have spines on tongue to snare prey

European hedgehog
if afraid, will curl into a ball with 6,000 spines sticking out

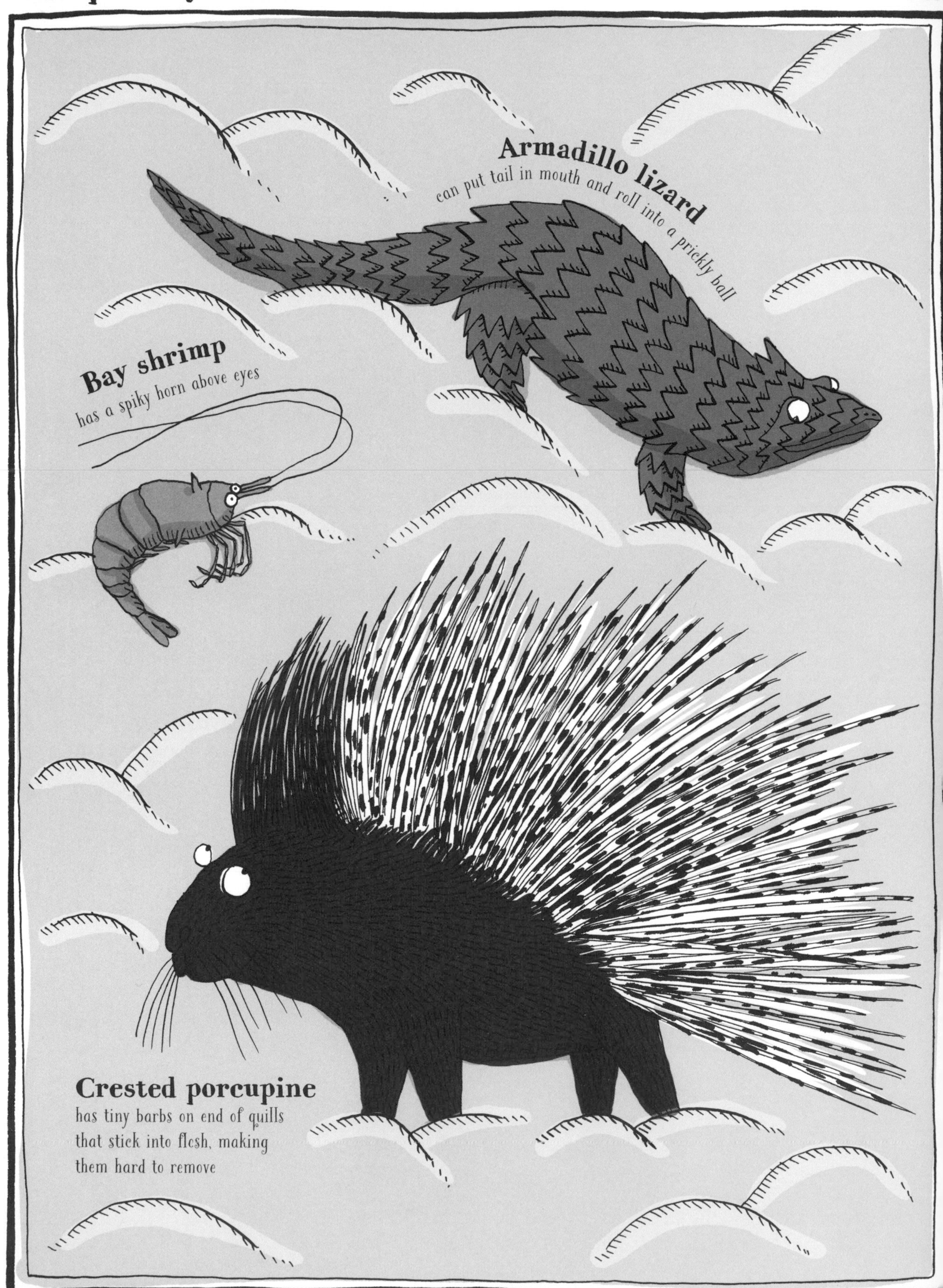
Armadillo lizard
can put tail in mouth and roll into a prickly ball
Bay shrimp
has a spiky horn above eyes
Crested porcupine
has tiny barbs on end of quills
that stick into flesh, making
them hard to remove

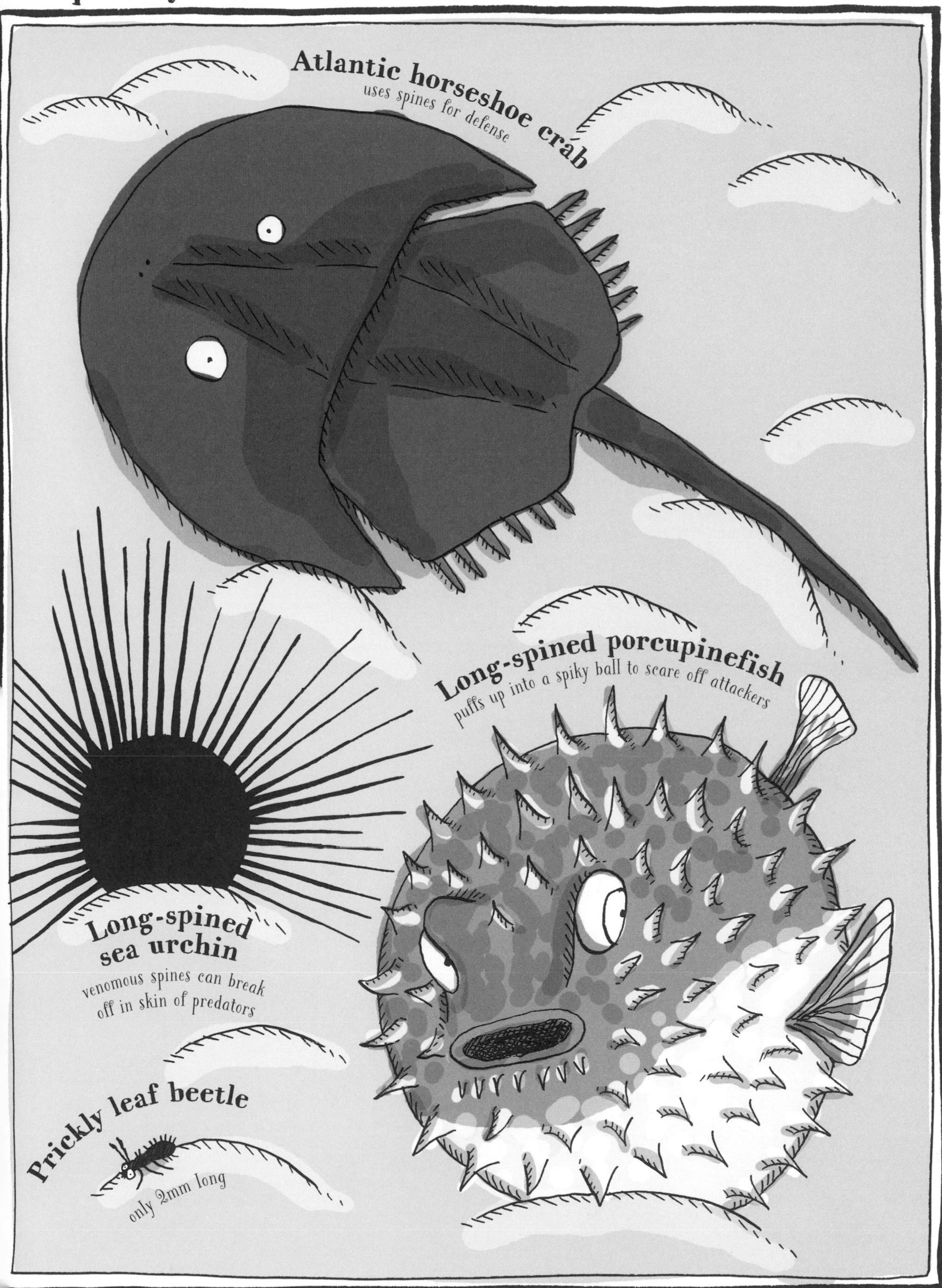
Atlantic horseshoe crab
uses spines for defense
Long-spined porcupinefish
puffs up into a spiky ball to scare off attackers
Long-spined sea urchin
venomous spines can break off in skin of predators
Prickly leaf beetle
only 2mm long

Horned desert viper
horns fold back to give snake smoother shape for burrowing
Horned lizard
puffs up and sticks out spikes to scare off attackers; can also squirt blood from eyes!

The redheads

Milk snake

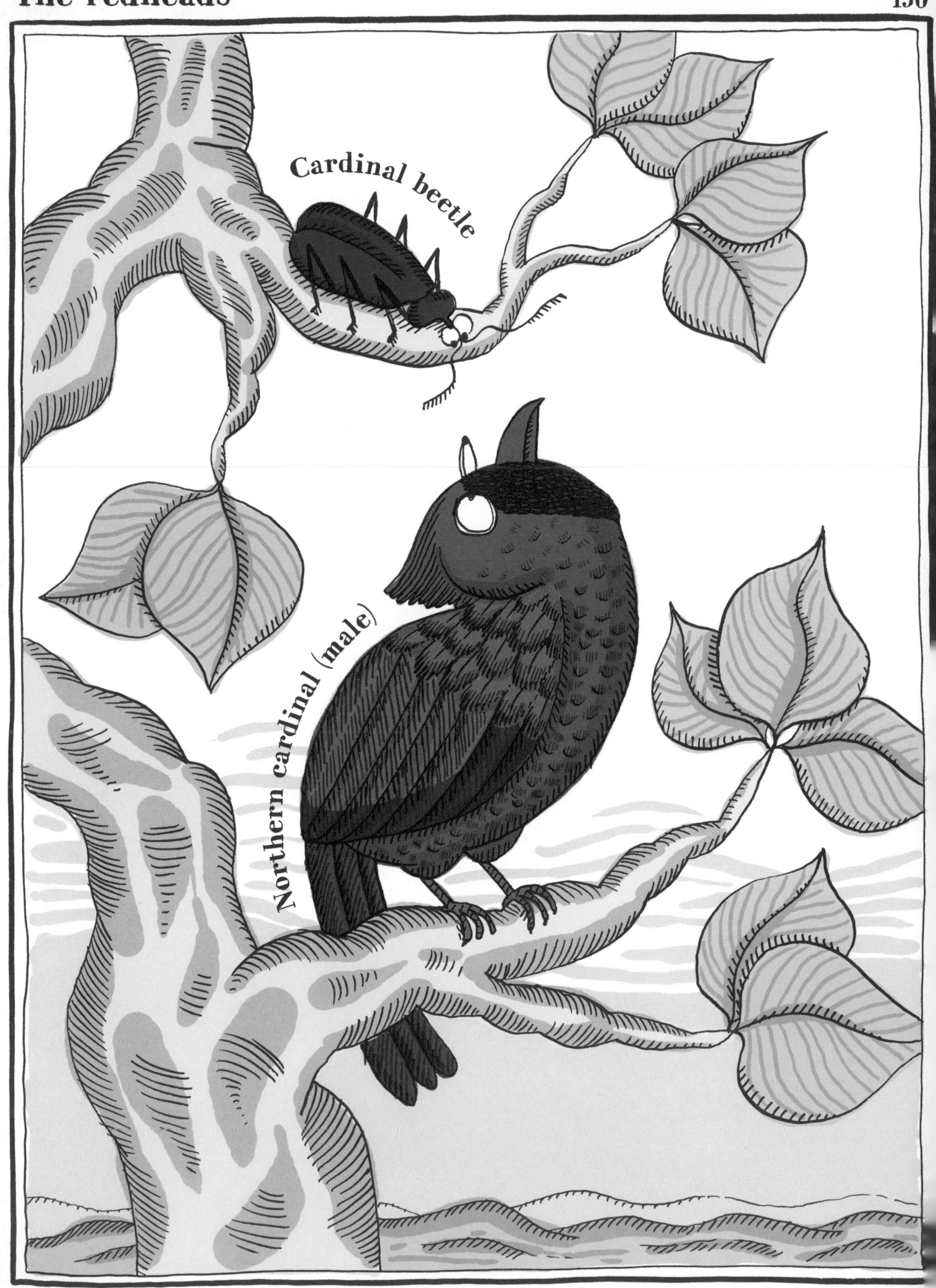
Cardinal beetle
Northern cardinal (male)

Crimson rosella
Scarlet tanager
Vermilion flycatcher

Poplar leaf beetle
Tomato frog
Orange roughy

Red weevil
Scarlet ibis
Firebug
Red salamander

The regal
Lion
Emperor scorpion

Golden eagle
Emperor angelfish

King snake
White tiger
Emperor penguin
Crowned sandgrouse

King cobra
Royal python

The show-offs

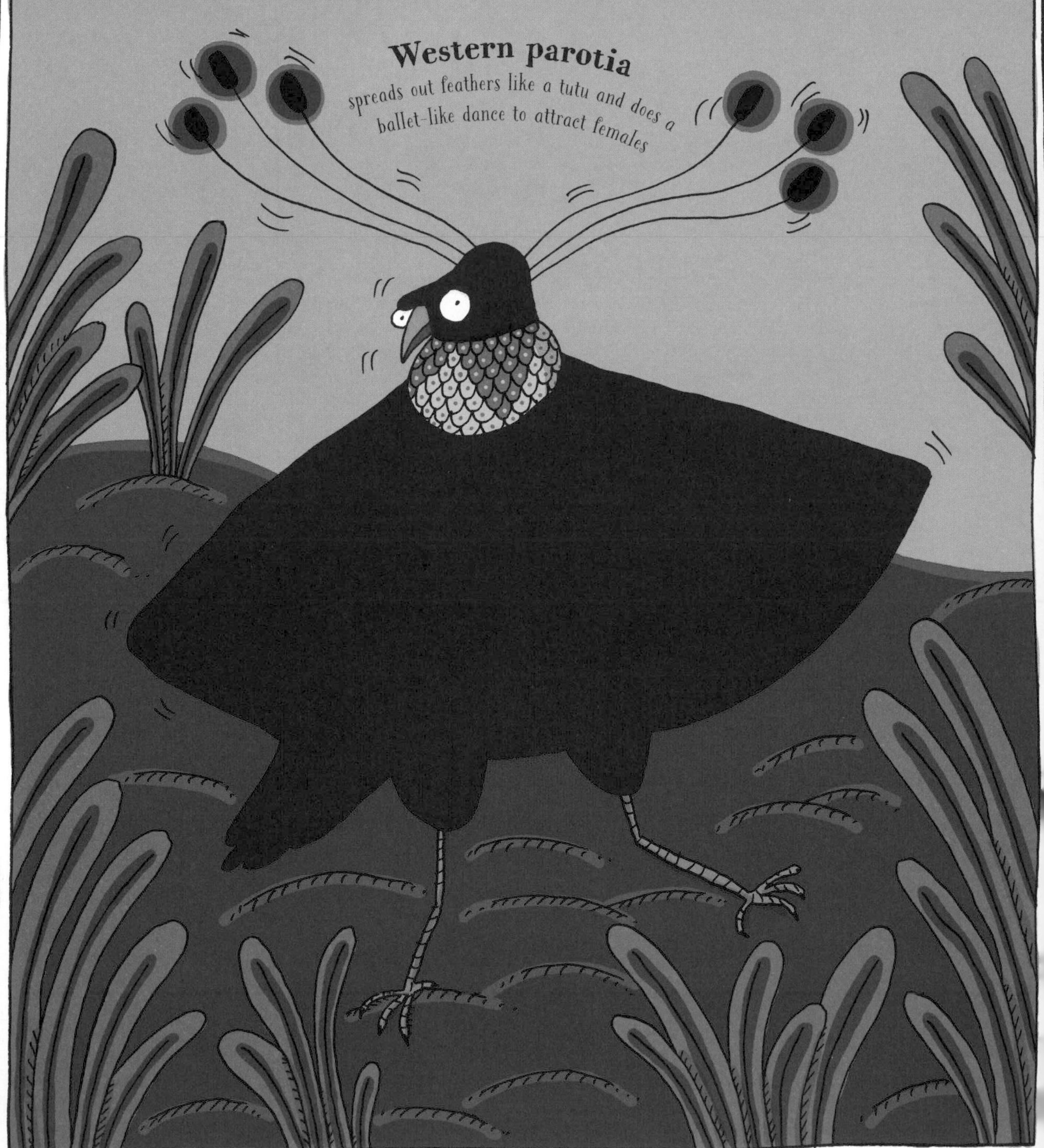

Western parotia
spreads out feathers like a tutu and does a ballet-like dance to attract females

Red-capped manakin
moonwalks along a branch to impress
Common pheasant
male circles female with tail fanned out
Satin bowerbird
male builds bower decorated with bright objects to attract a mate
Marten
male chases female through the trees

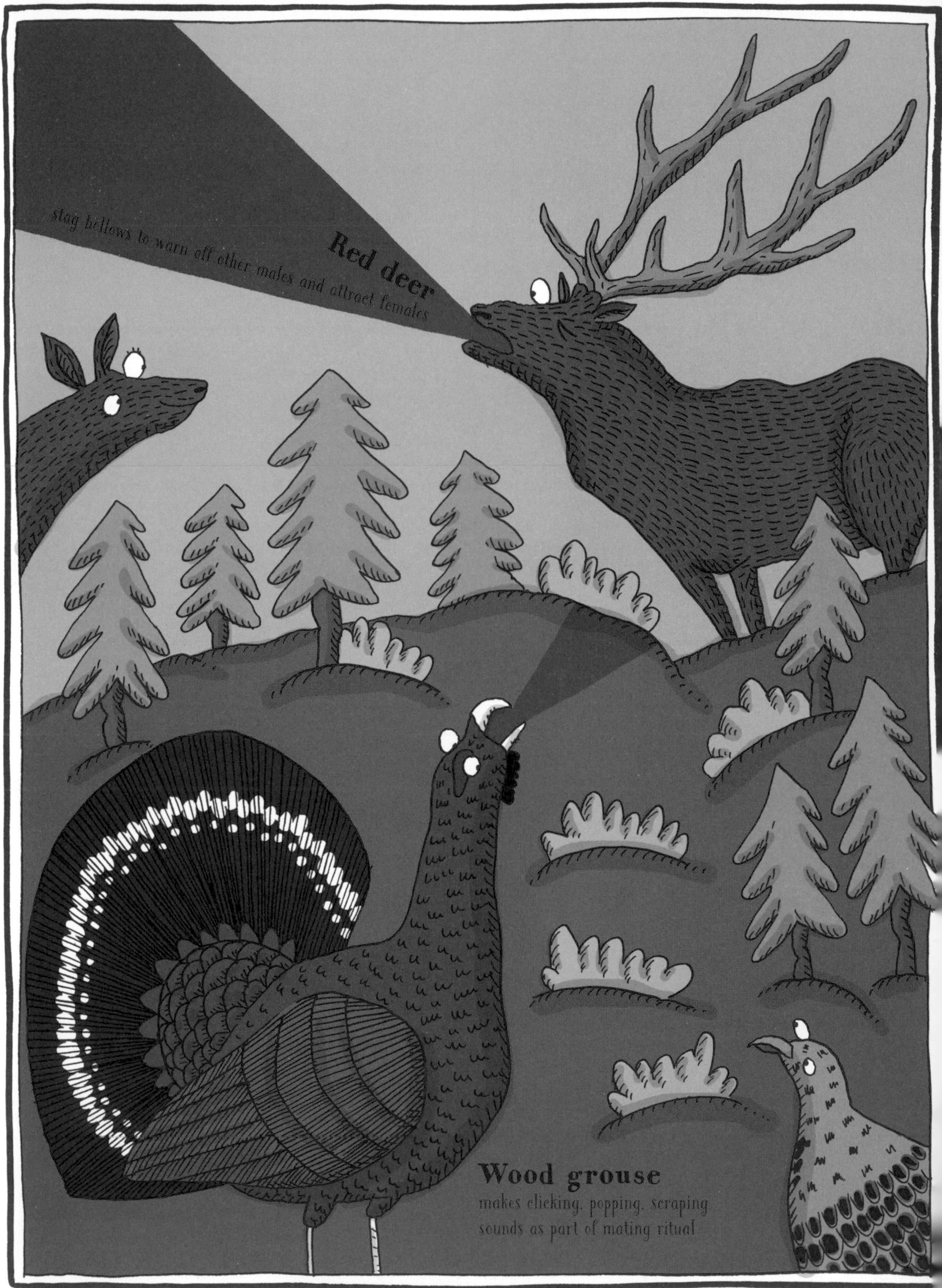
Red deer
stag bellows to warn off other males and attract females
Wood grouse
makes clicking, popping, scraping sounds as part of mating ritual

Superb lyrebird
male fans tail, dances, and sings to impress a mate
Magnificent frigate bird
male puffs up red throat-pouch like a balloon

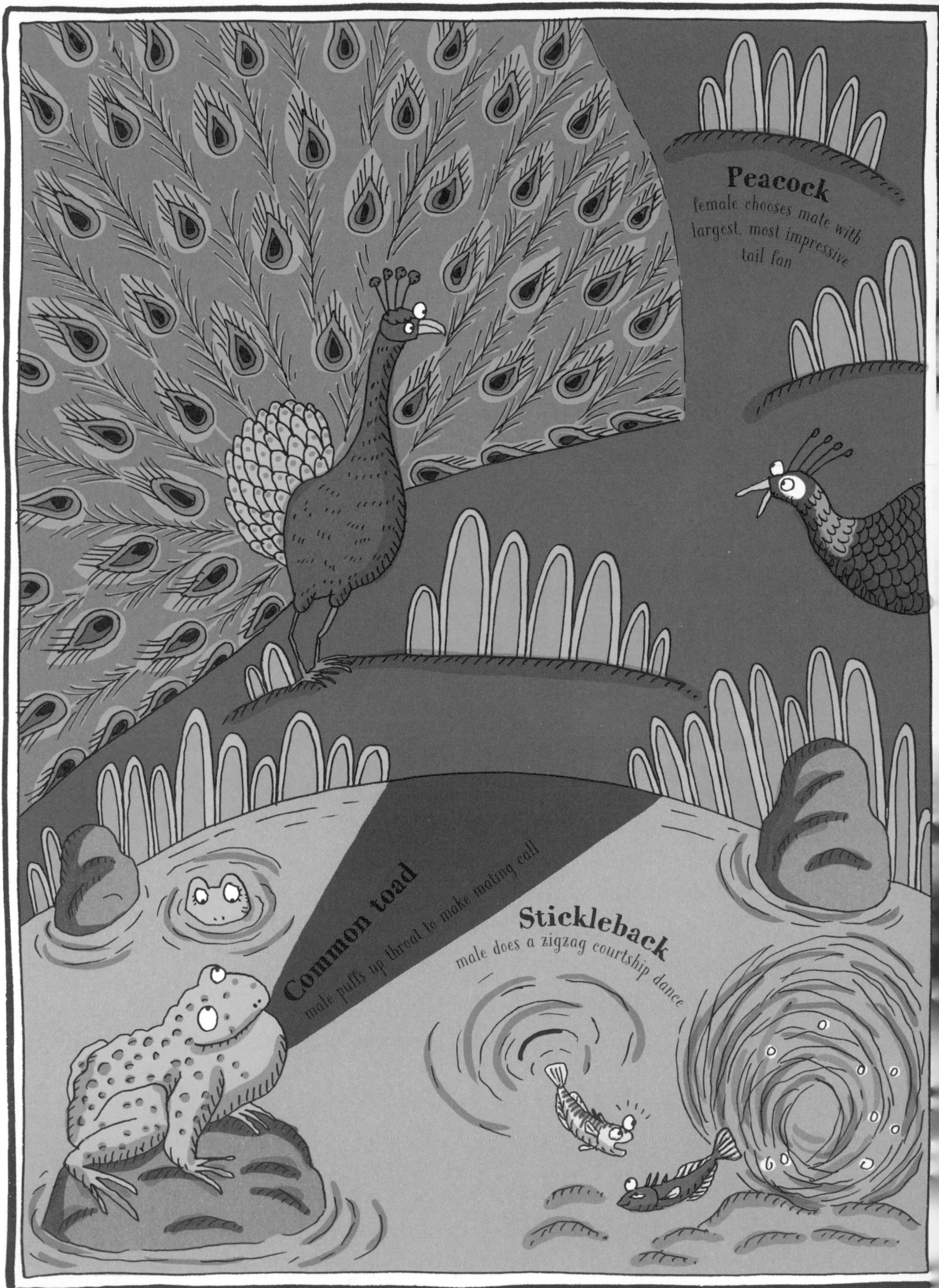
Peacock
female chooses mate with largest, most impressive tail fan
Common toad
male puffs up throat to make mating call
Stickleback
male does a zigzag courtship dance

Toco toucan
male offers female gifts of food
Gray-crowned crane
bows, jumps, and dances

The snowy-whites

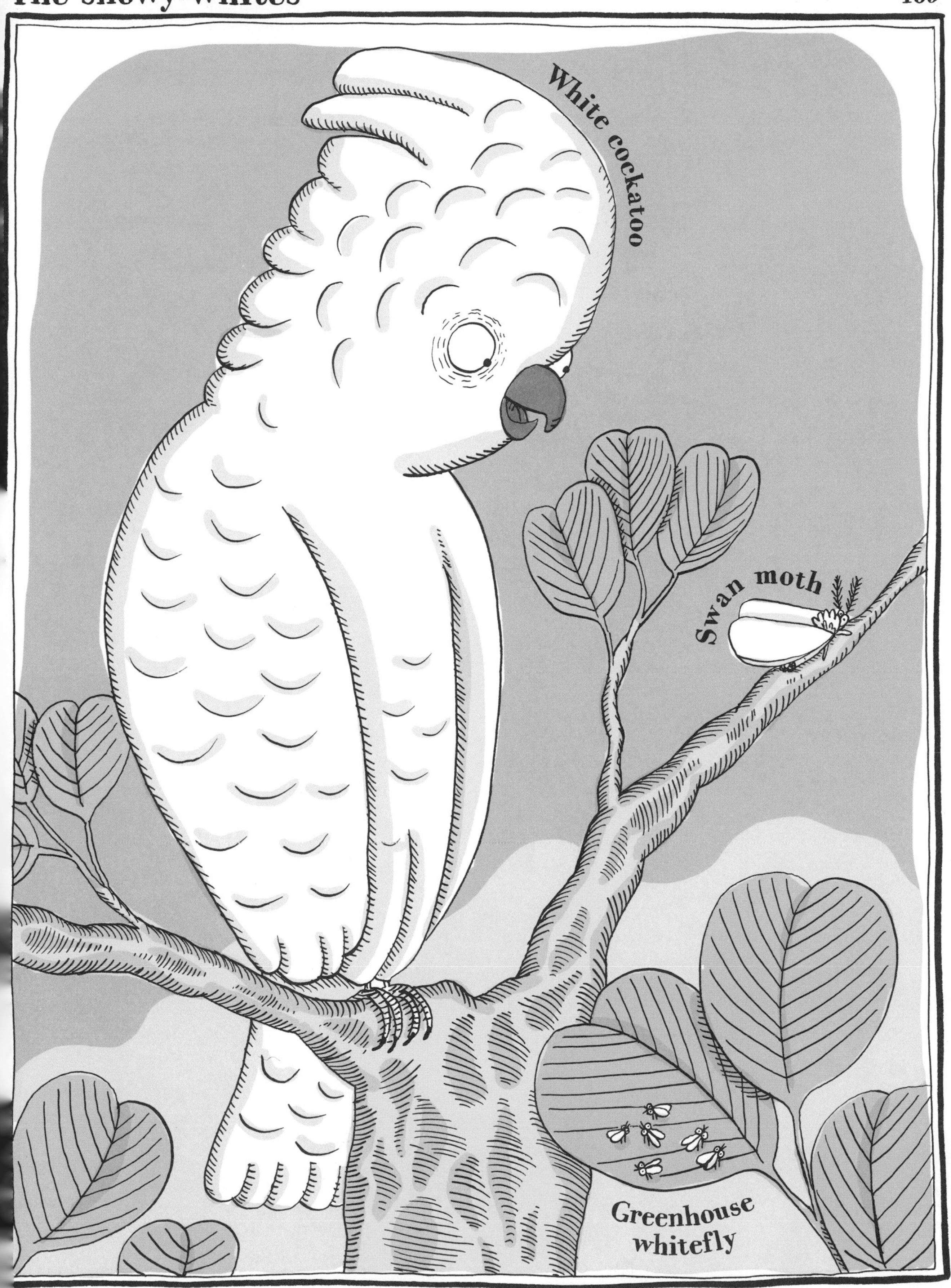
White cockatoo
Swan moth
Greenhouse whitefly

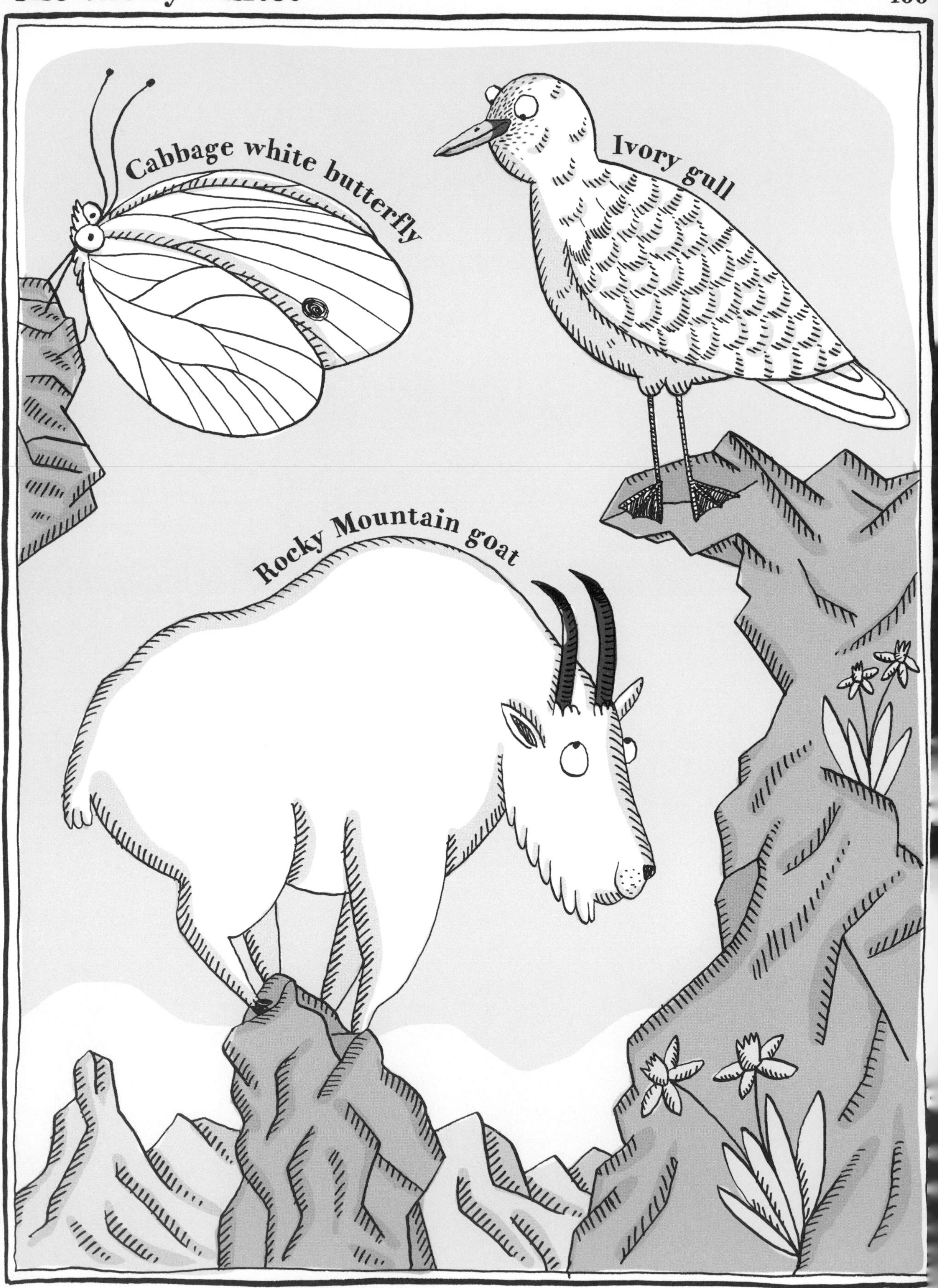
Cabbage white butterfly
Ivory gull
Rocky Mountain goat

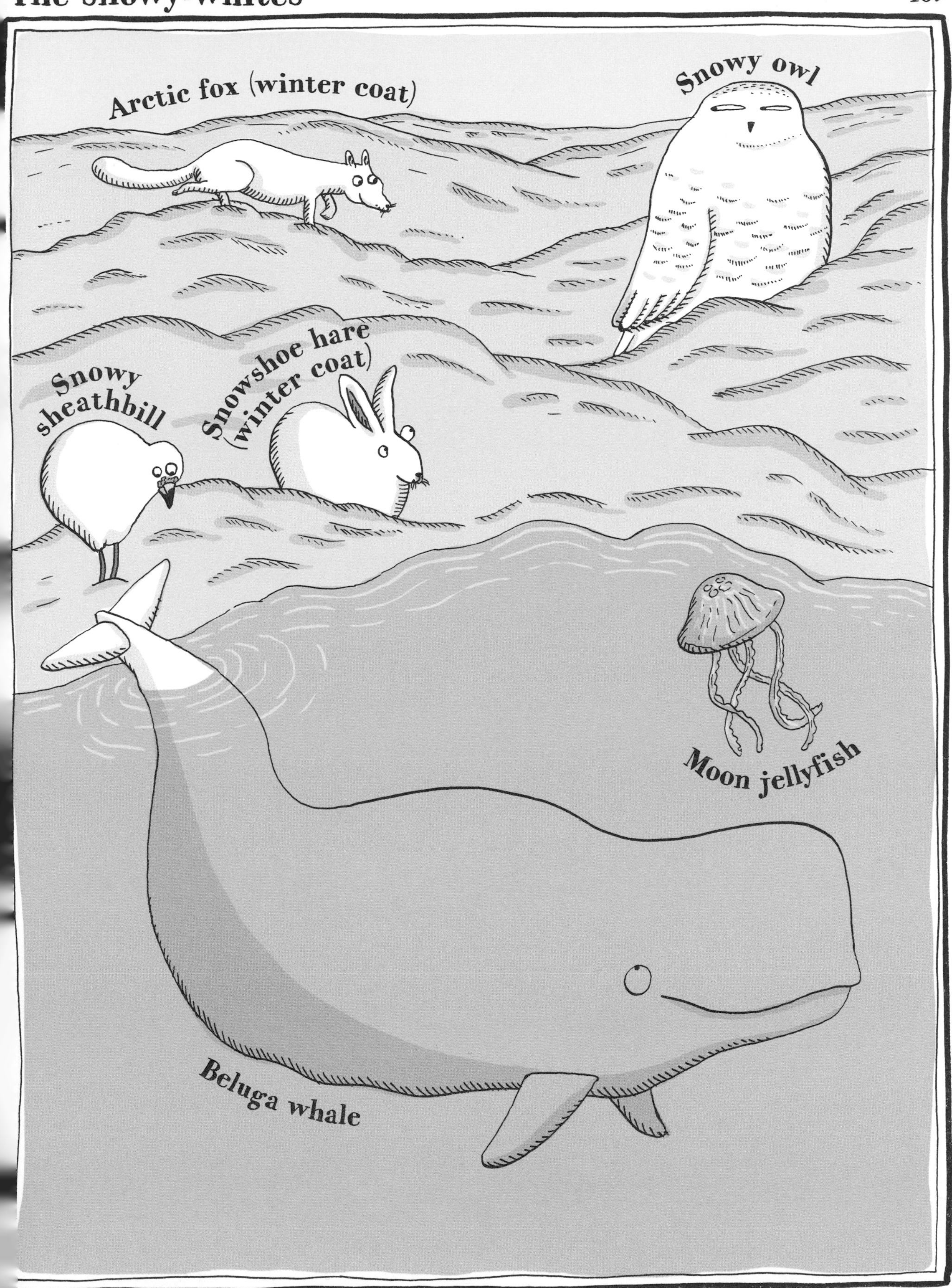
Arctic fox (winter coat)
Snowy owl
Snowy sheathbill
Snowshoe hare (winter coat)
Moon jellyfish
Beluga whale

The solitary

Black vulture

Brown bear

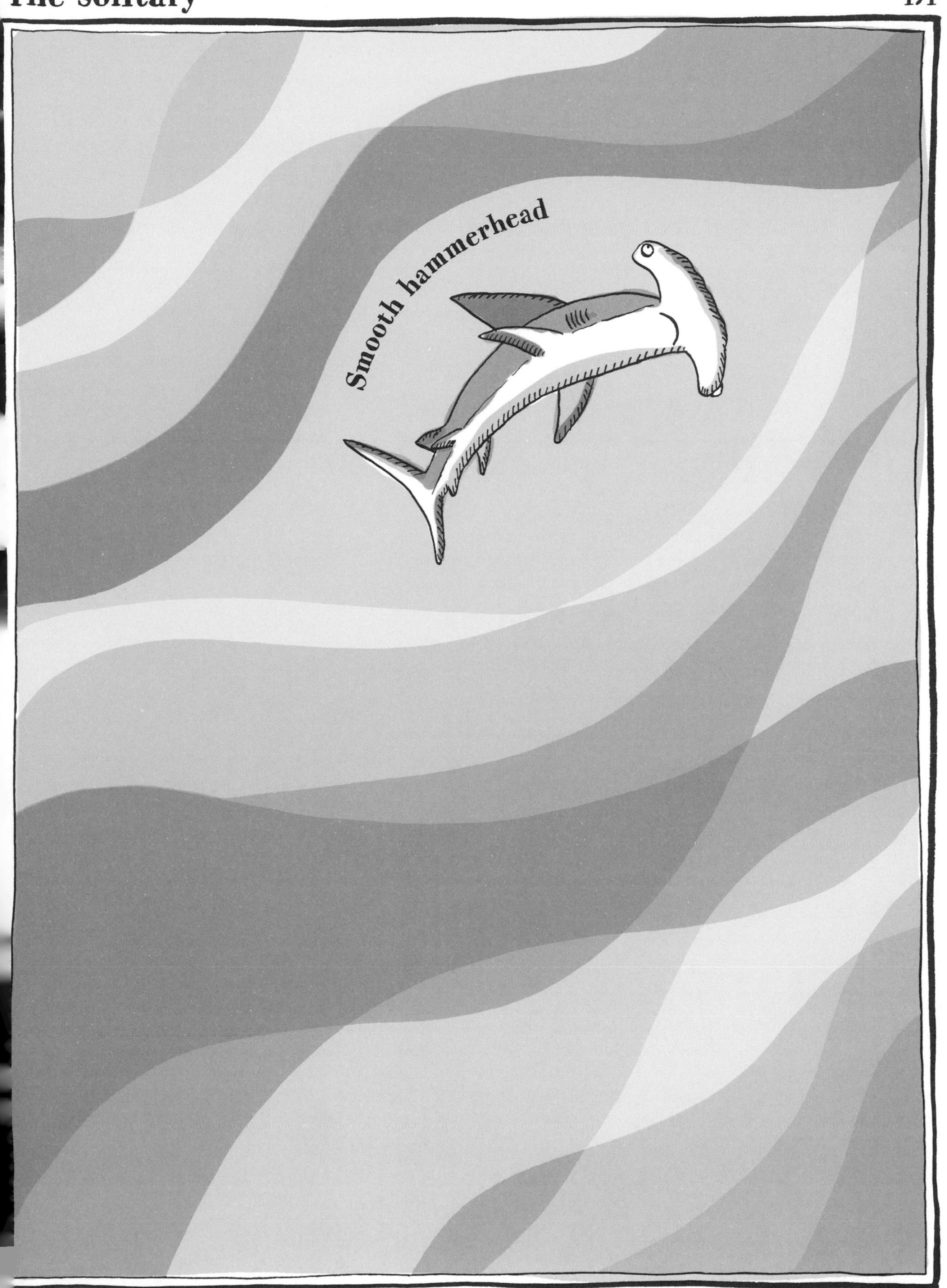
Smooth hammerhead

Giant grouper

Praying mantis

The solitary

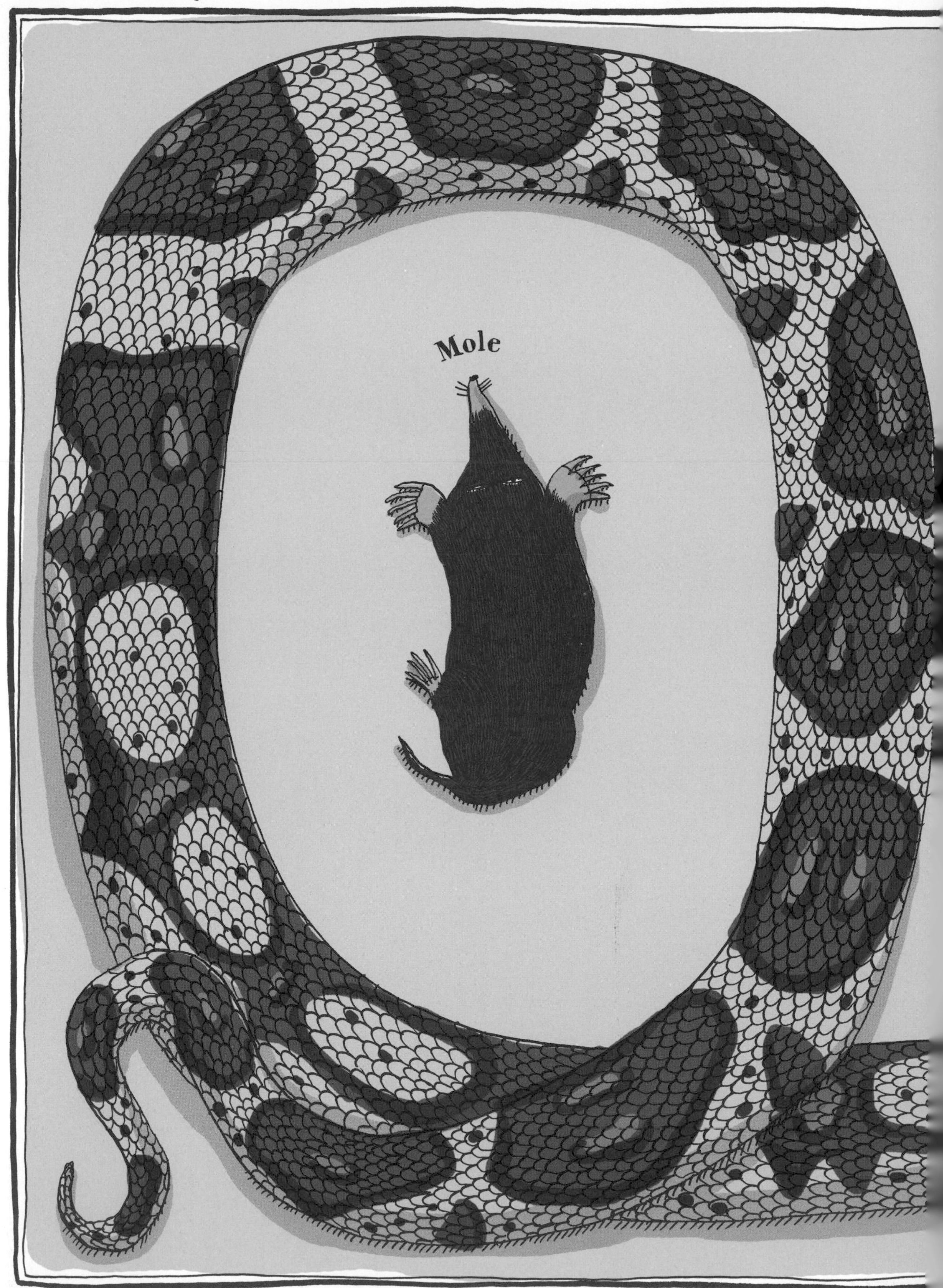

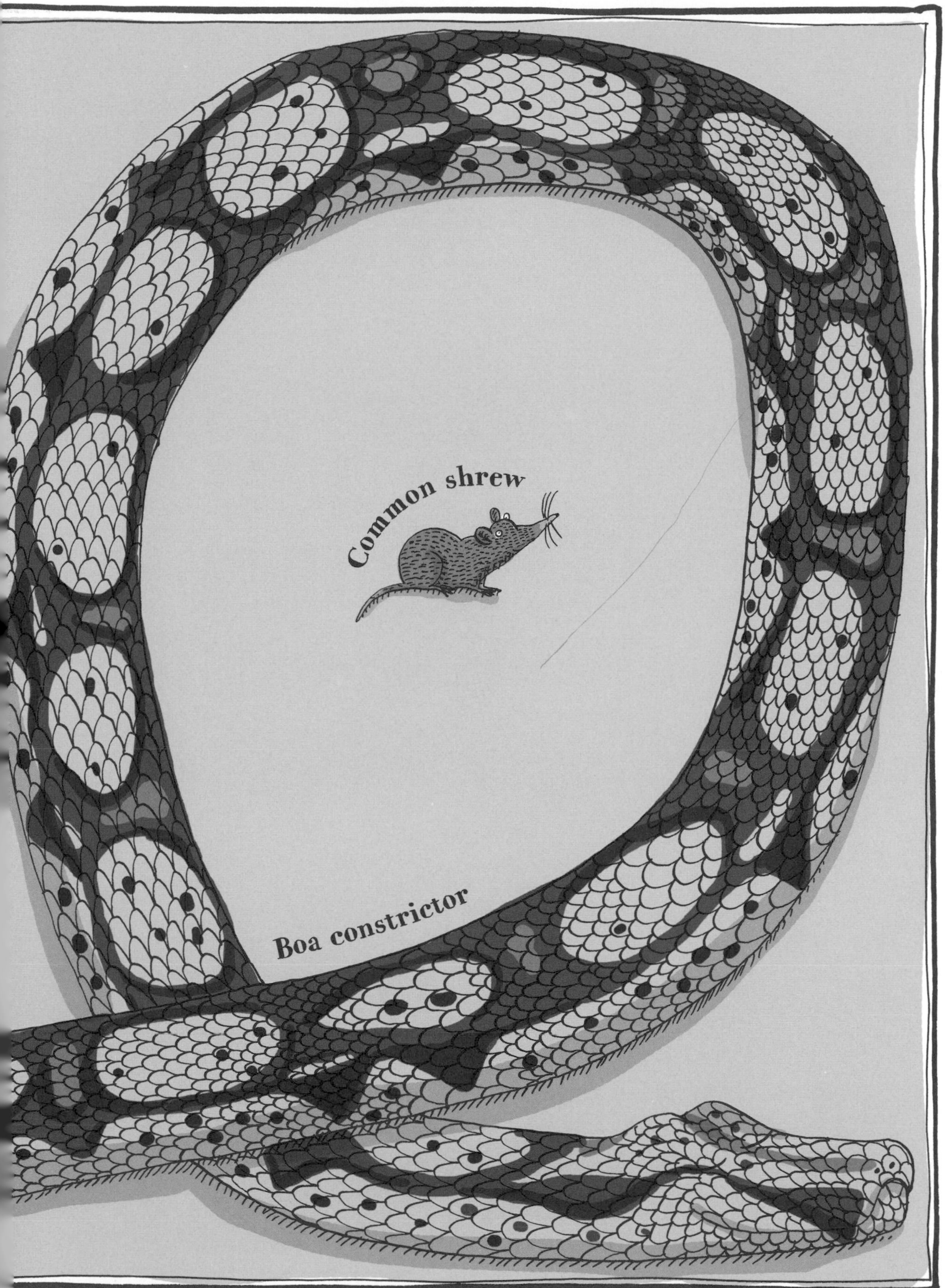
Common shrew
Boa constrictor

Siamese fighting fish

Leopard
Digger wasp

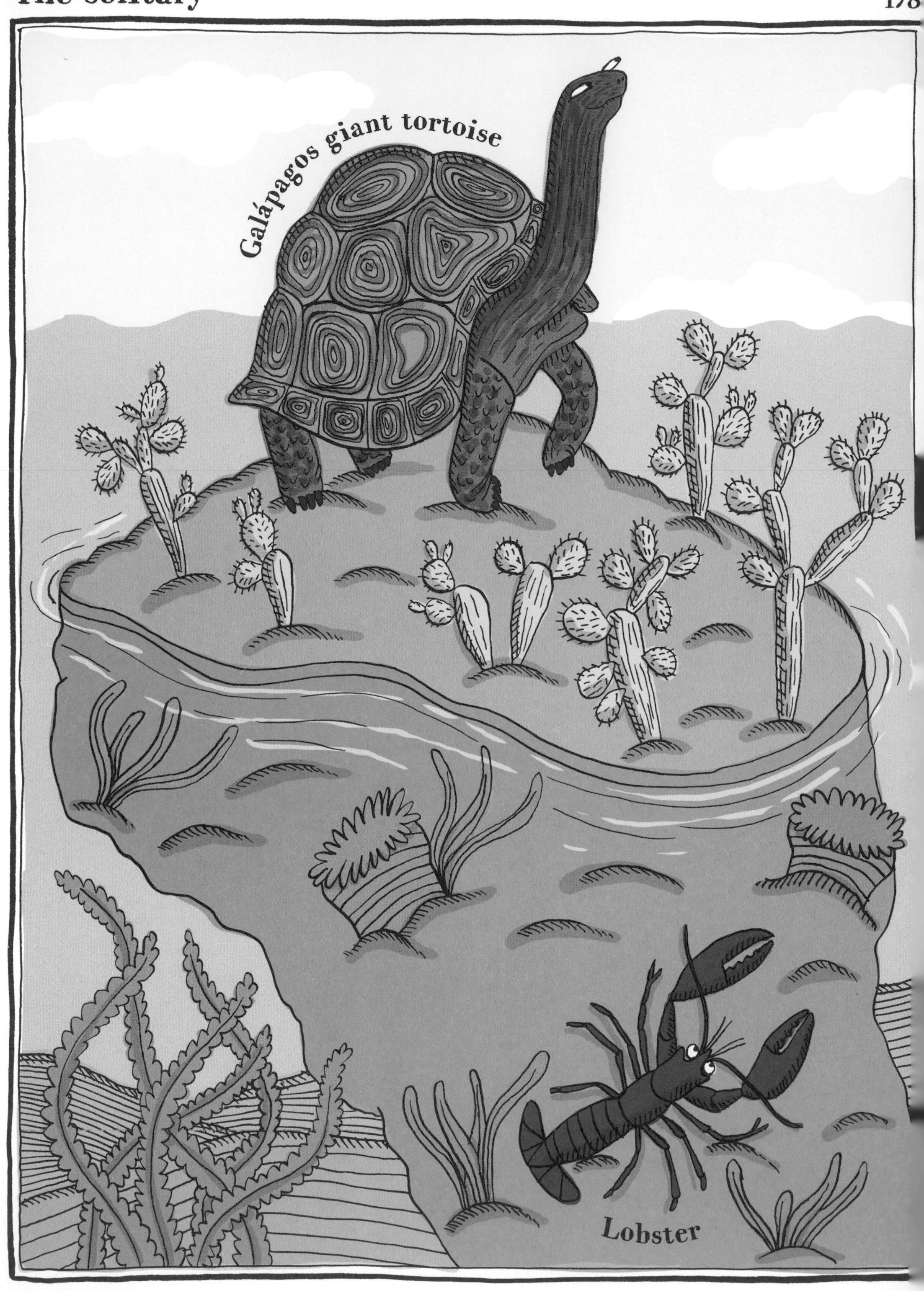
Galápagos giant tortoise
Lobster

The spotted

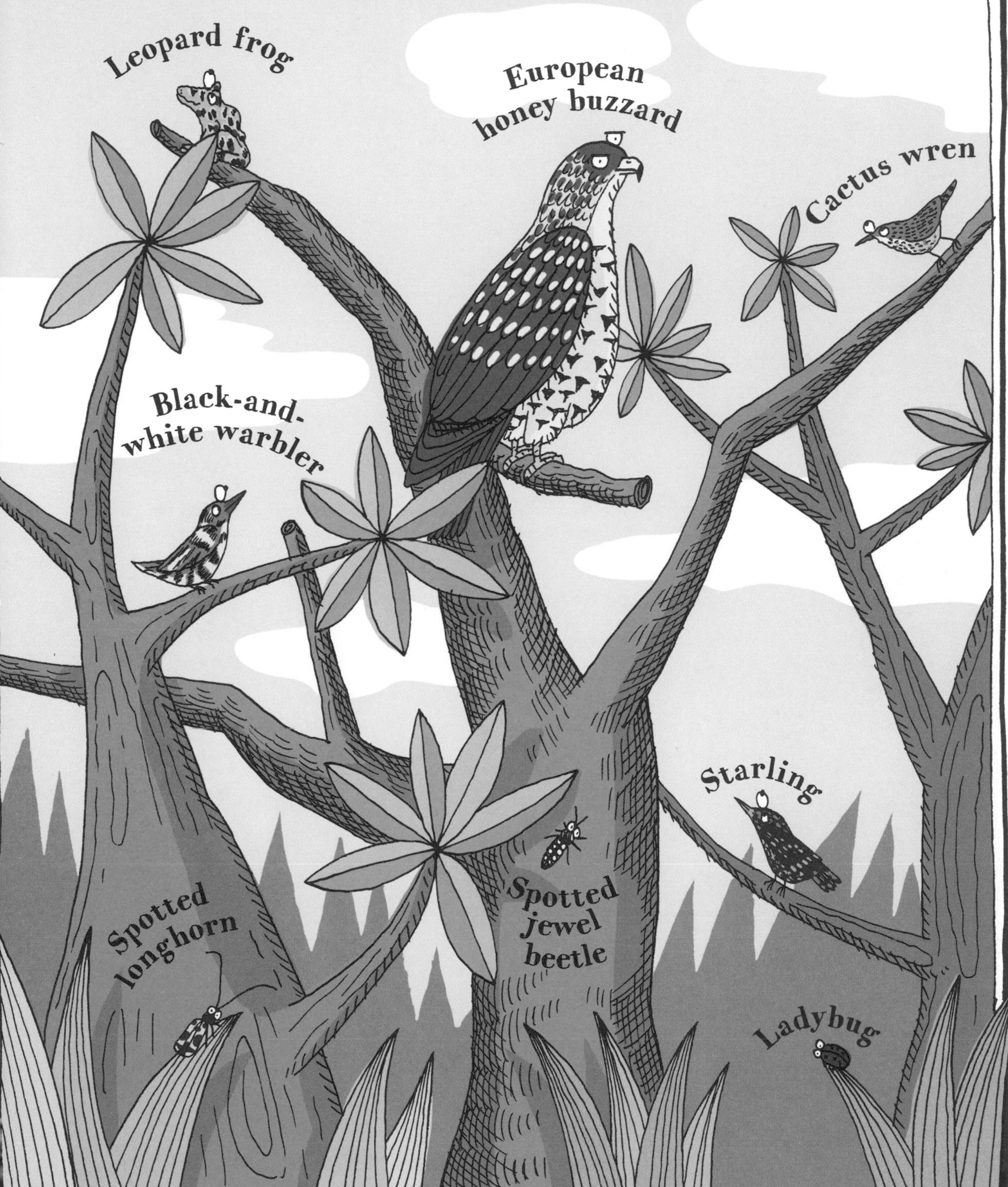

Leopard frog
European honey buzzard
Cactus wren
Black-and-white warbler
Starling
Spotted longhorn
Spotted jewel beetle
Ladybug

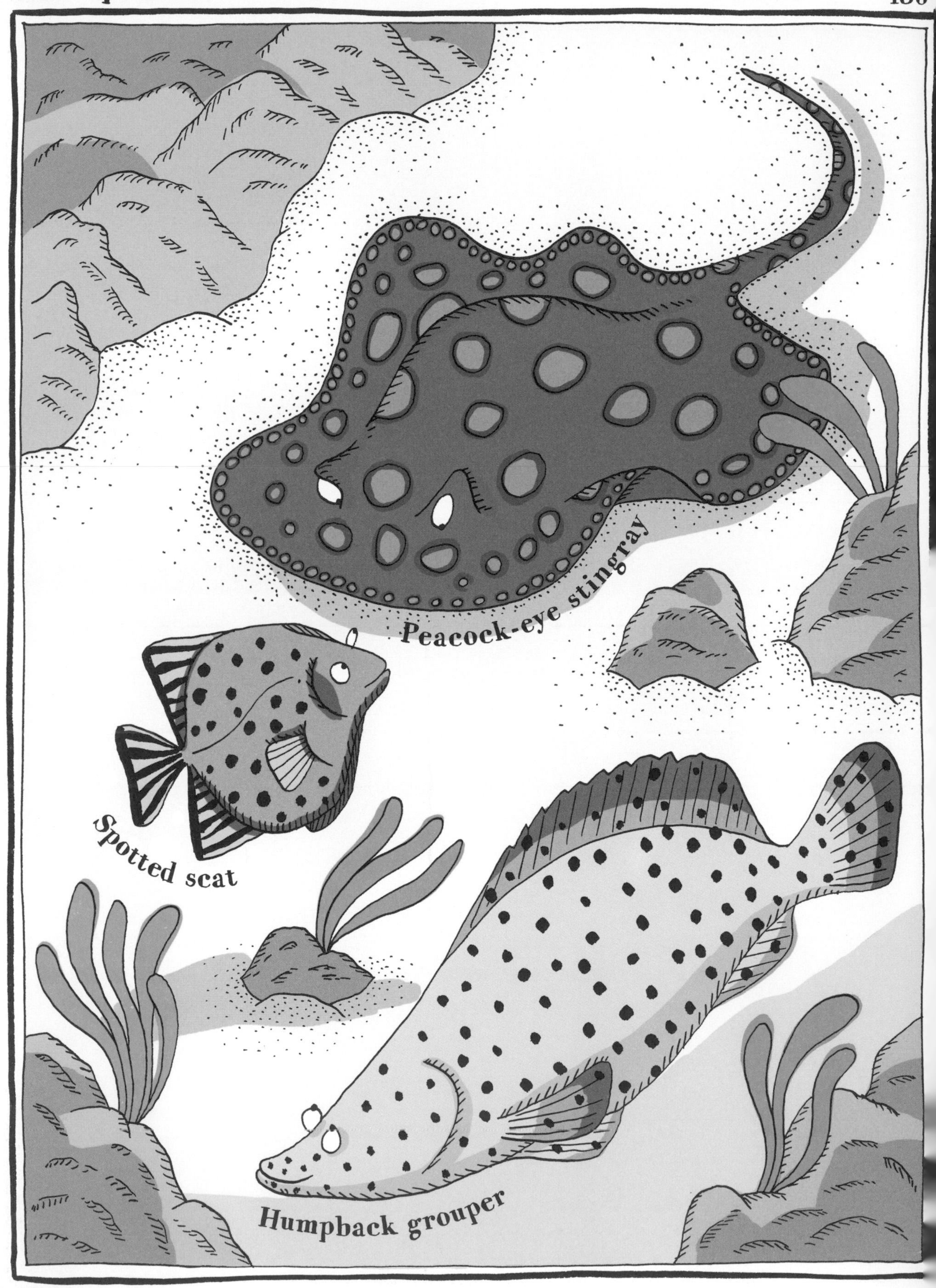
Peacock-eye stingray
Spotted scat
Humpback grouper

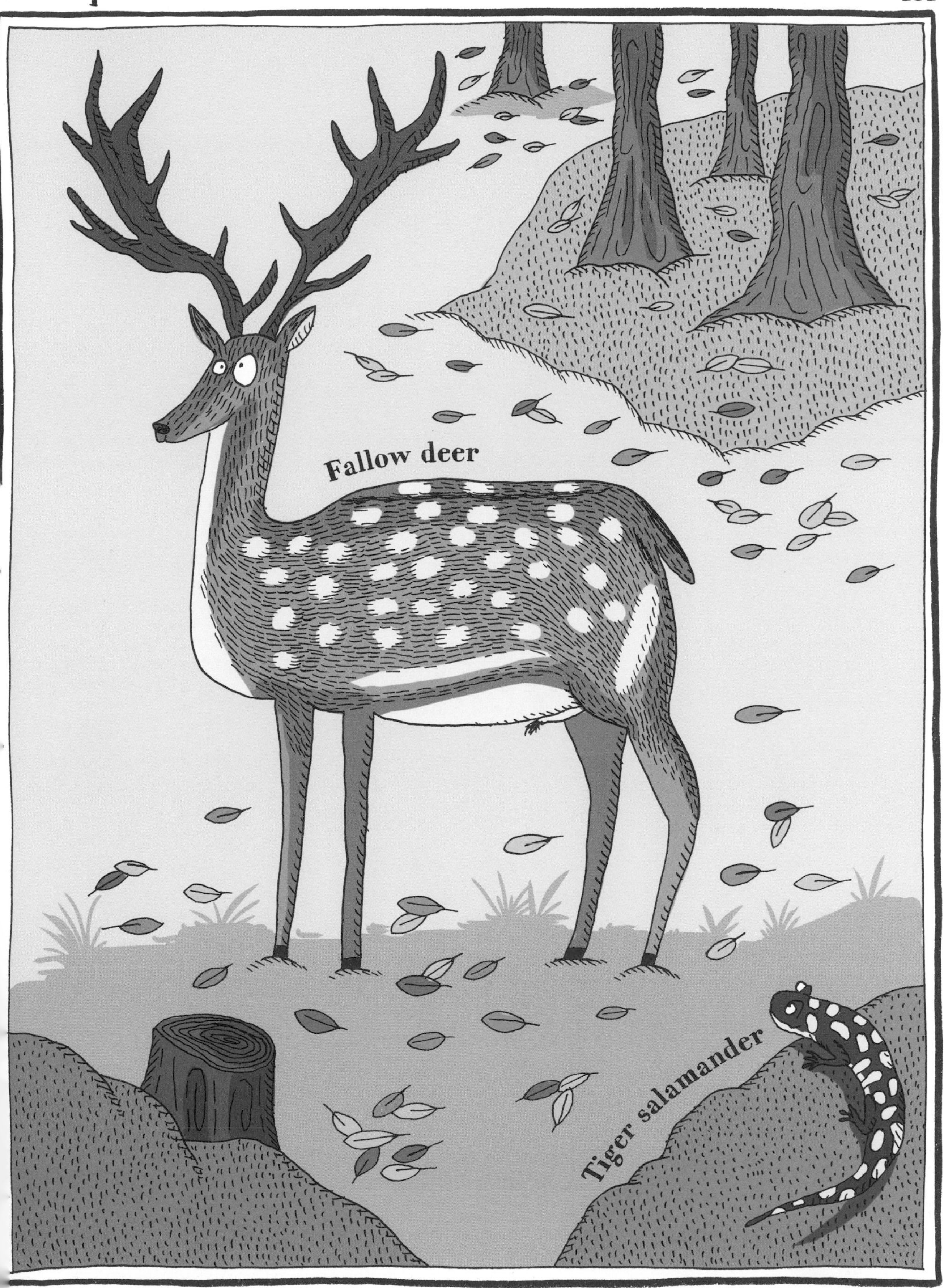
Fallow deer
Tiger salamander

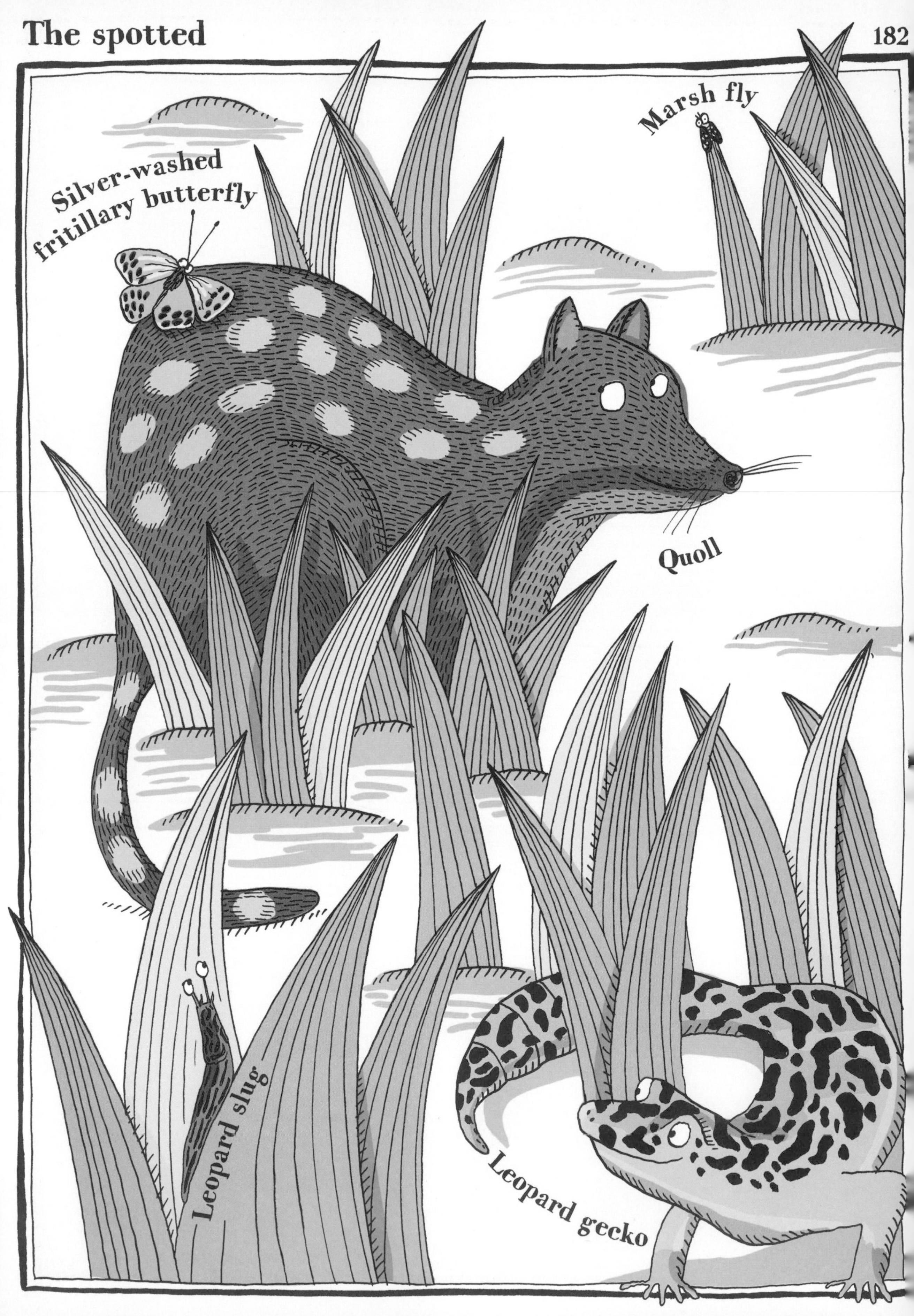
Silver-washed
fritillary butterfly
Marsh fly
Quoll
Leopard slug
Leopard gecko

The sprinters

Peregrine falcon
up to 242 mph
Moose
up to
35 mph
Common
noctule
up to 31 mph

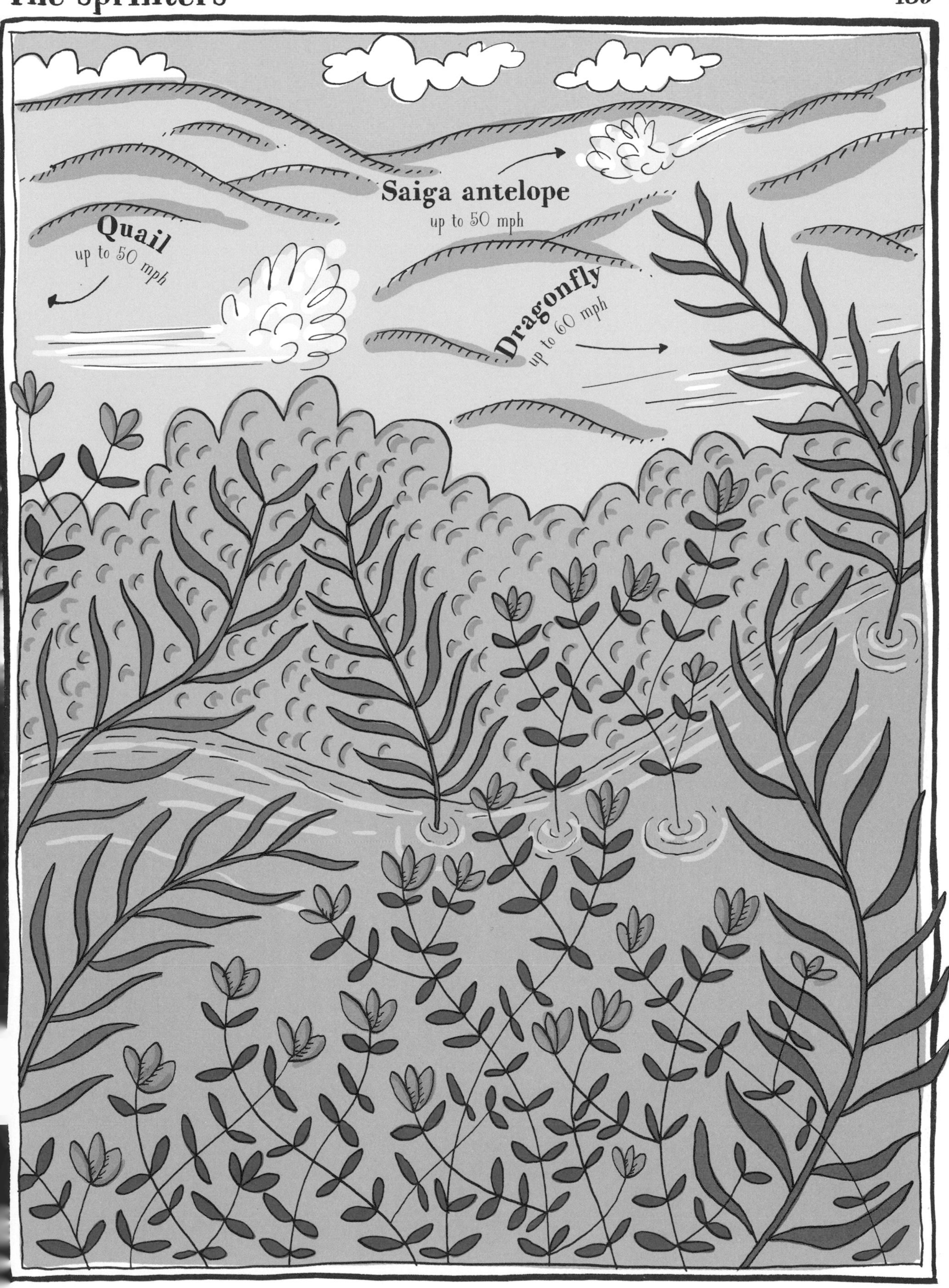
Saiga antelope
up to 50 mph
Quail
up to 50 mph
Dragonfly
up to 60 mph

The sprinters

Common ostrich
up to 43 mph
Rhinoceros
up to 30 mph
Greater roadrunner
up to 26 mph

The striped

Aardwolf

Striped hyena

Moorish idol
Copperband butterfly fish
Sheepshead

Fiji banded iguana
Bandy-bandy
Banded sea krait

Leopard ground squirrel
Barred antshrike
Numbat
Banded mongoose

Scarce swallowtail butterfly

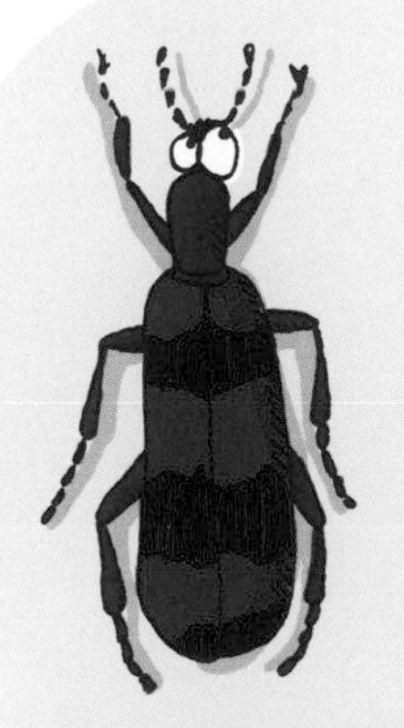

Checkered beetle

Striped cucumber beetle

Minstrel bug

Colorado potato beetle

The unlucky
Rock dove
believed to carry diseases

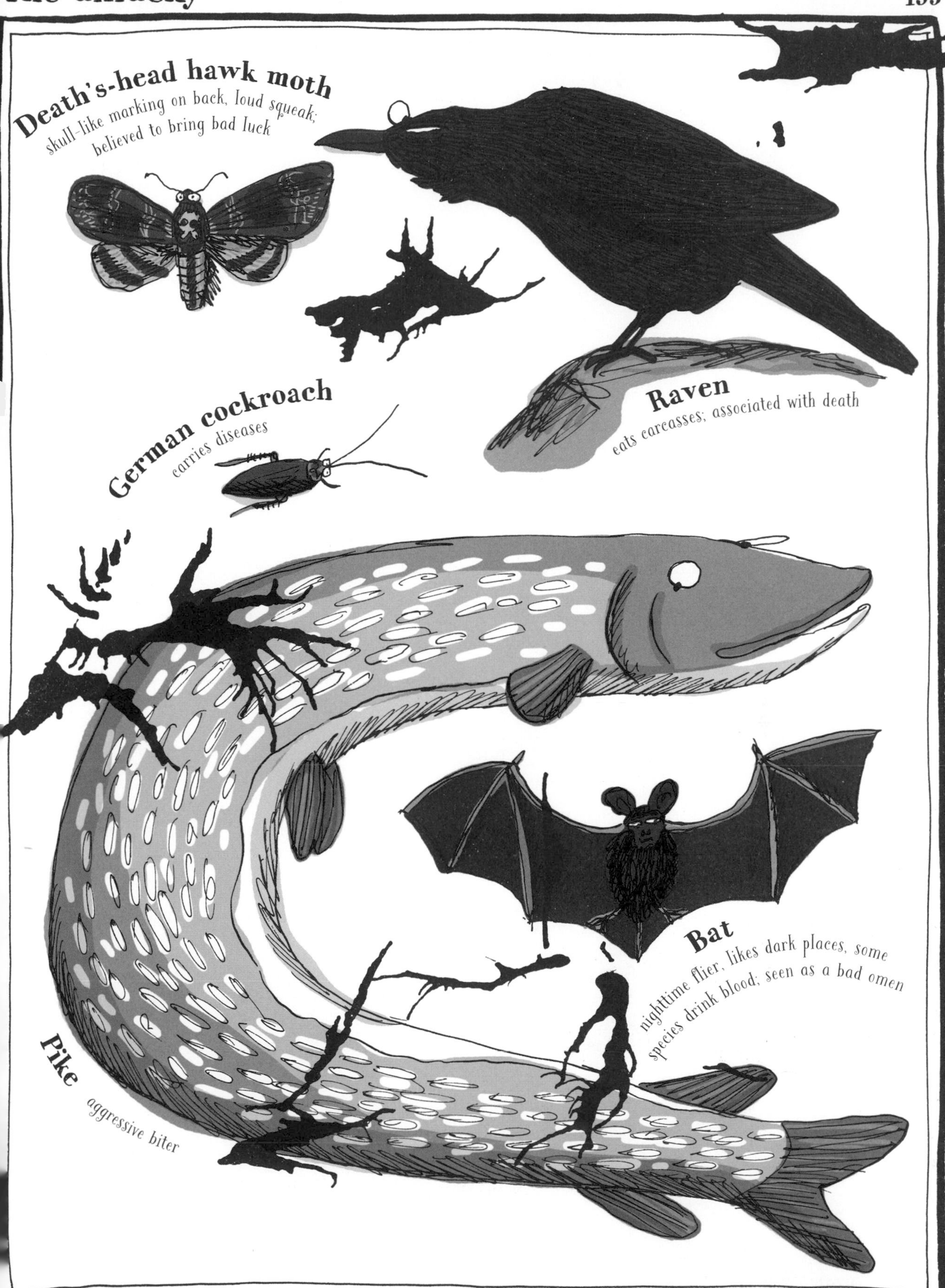
Death's-head hawk moth
skull-like marking on back, loud squeak; believed to bring bad luck
Raven
eats carcasses; associated with death
German cockroach
carries diseases
Bat
nighttime flier, likes dark places, some species drink blood; seen as a bad omen
Pike
aggressive biter

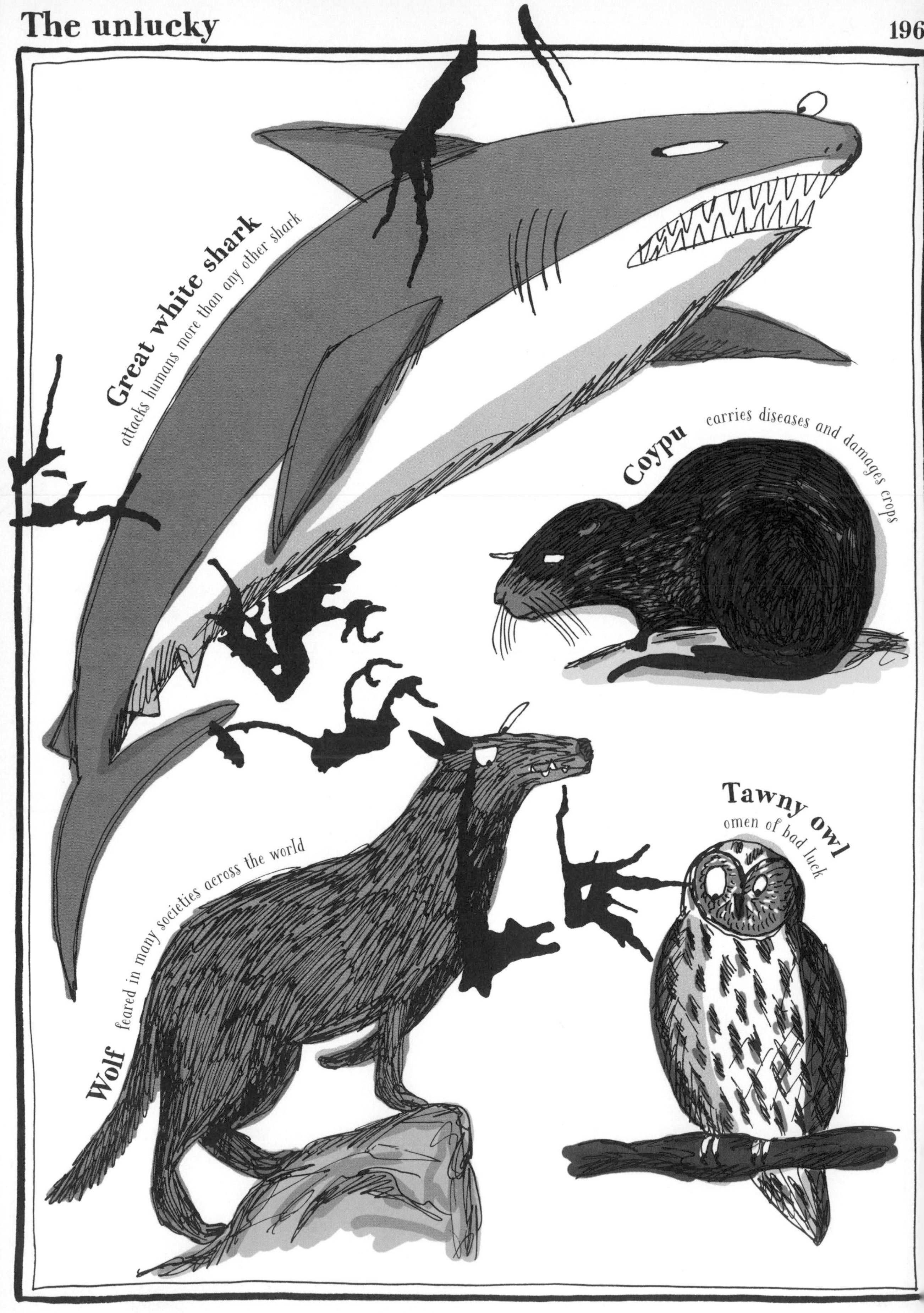
Great white shark
attacks humans more than any other shark
Coypu
carries diseases and damages crops
Wolf
feared in many societies across the world
Tawny owl
omen of bad luck

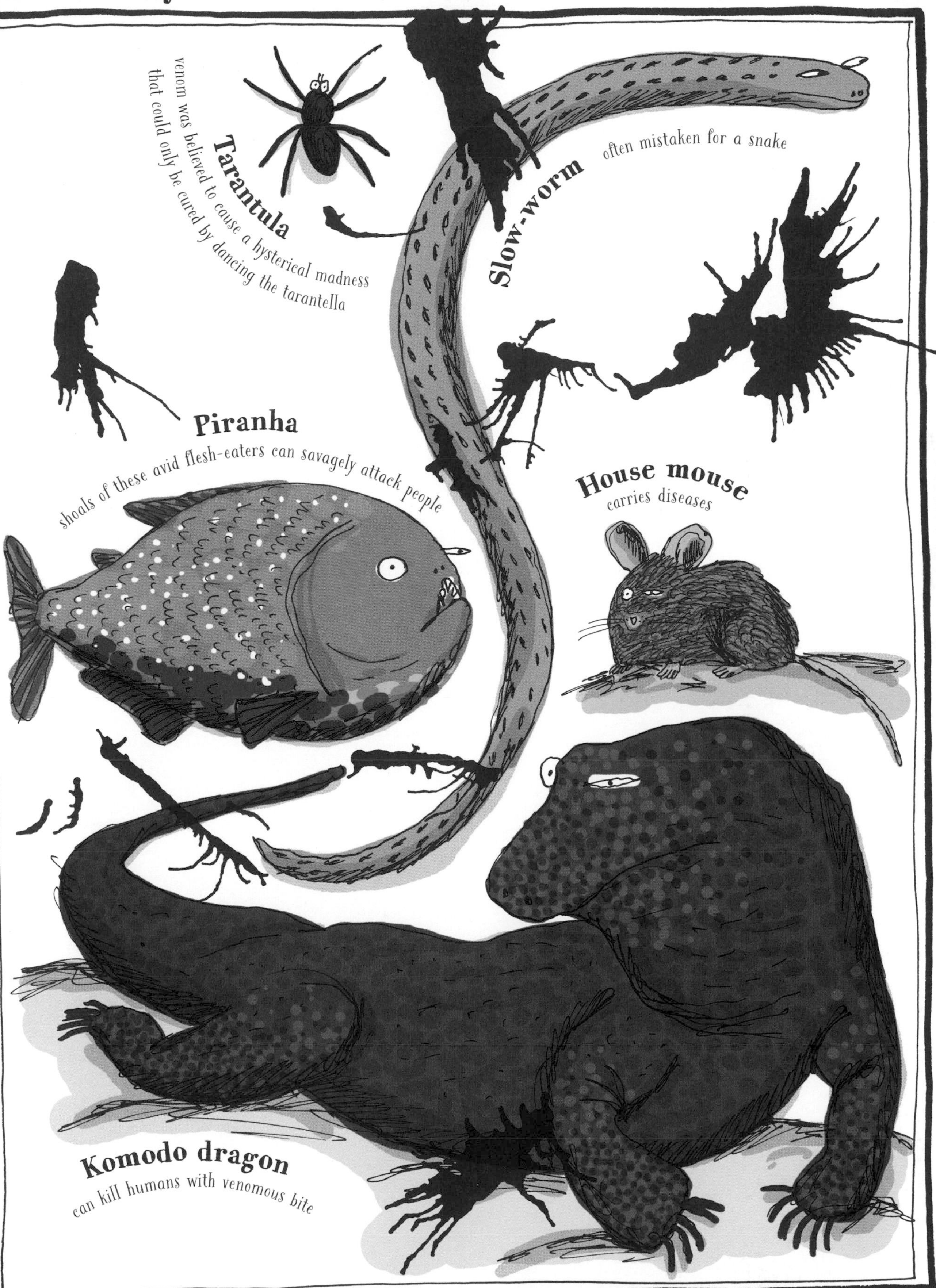
Tarantula
venom was believed to cause a hysterical madness that could only be cured by dancing the tarantella
Slow-worm
often mistaken for a snake
Piranha
shoals of these avid flesh-eaters can savagely attack people
House mouse
carries diseases
Komodo dragon
can kill humans with venomous bite

Hoopoe
seen as an omen of war or death in some cultures
Fire salamander
said to be able to withstand flames
Earwig
said to pierce the eardrums of sleepers
Brown rat
carries diseases

The vanished

Steller's sea cow
† 1768
Baiji
† 2006
Mammoth
† 12,000 years ago
Pig-footed bandicoot
† 1907

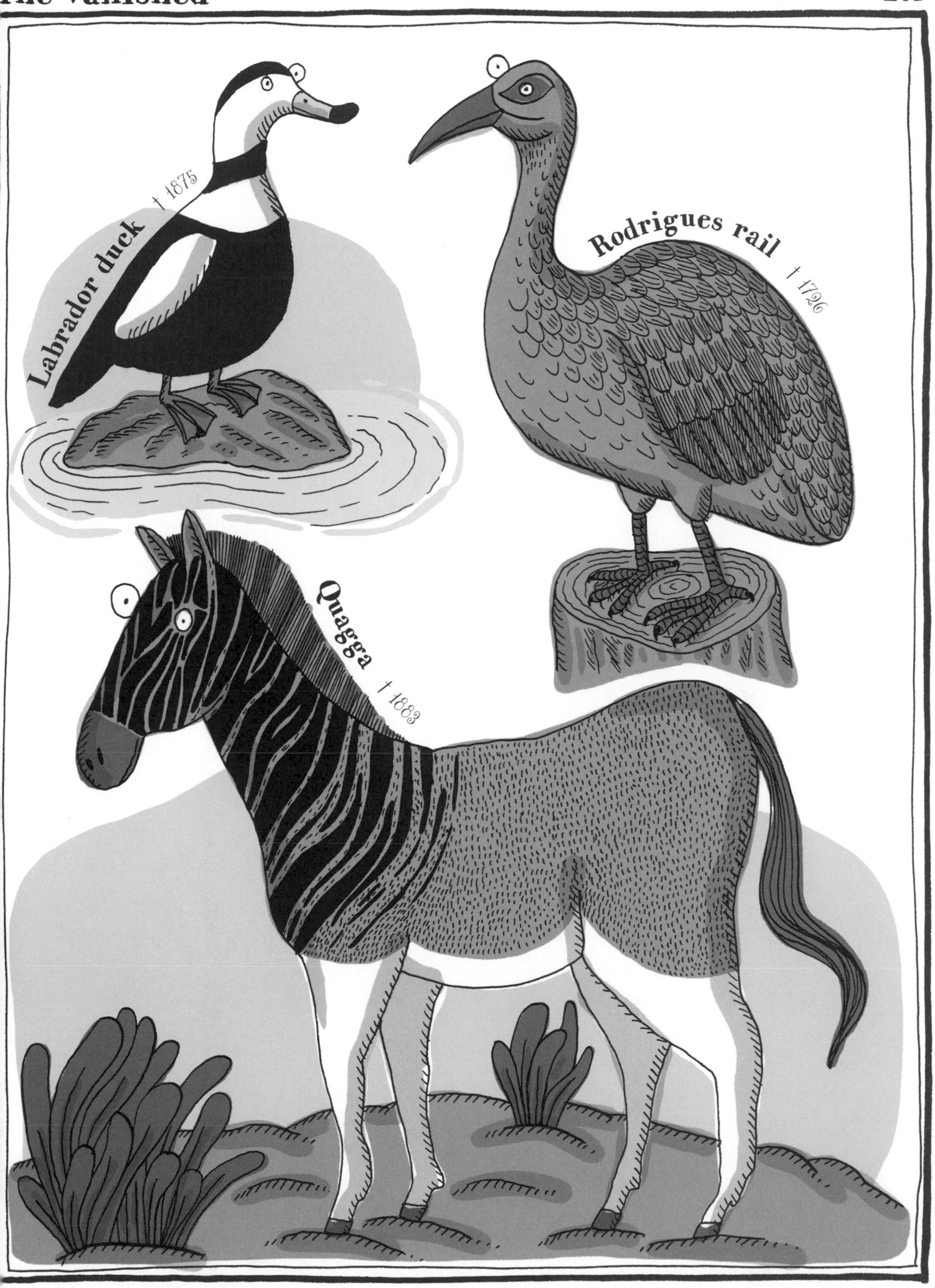
Labrador duck
† 1875
Rodrigues rail
† 1726
Quagga
† 1883

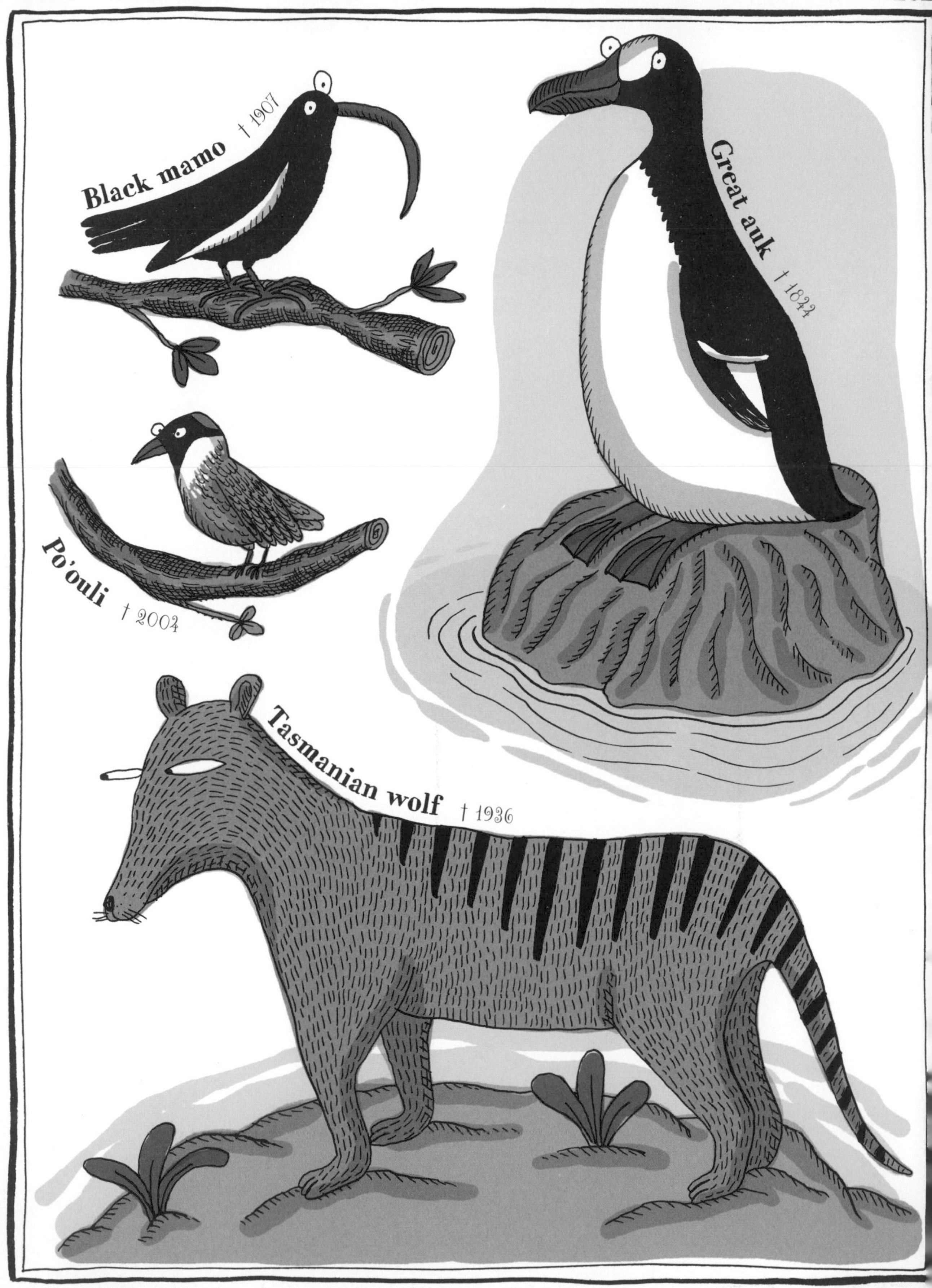
Black mamo † 1907
Great auk † 1844
Po'ouli † 2004
Tasmanian wolf † 1936

Dinosaurs

† 65 million years ago

The voyagers

Common frog
travels to lay eggs

Blue wildebeest
migrates up to 1,000 miles each year within east Africa

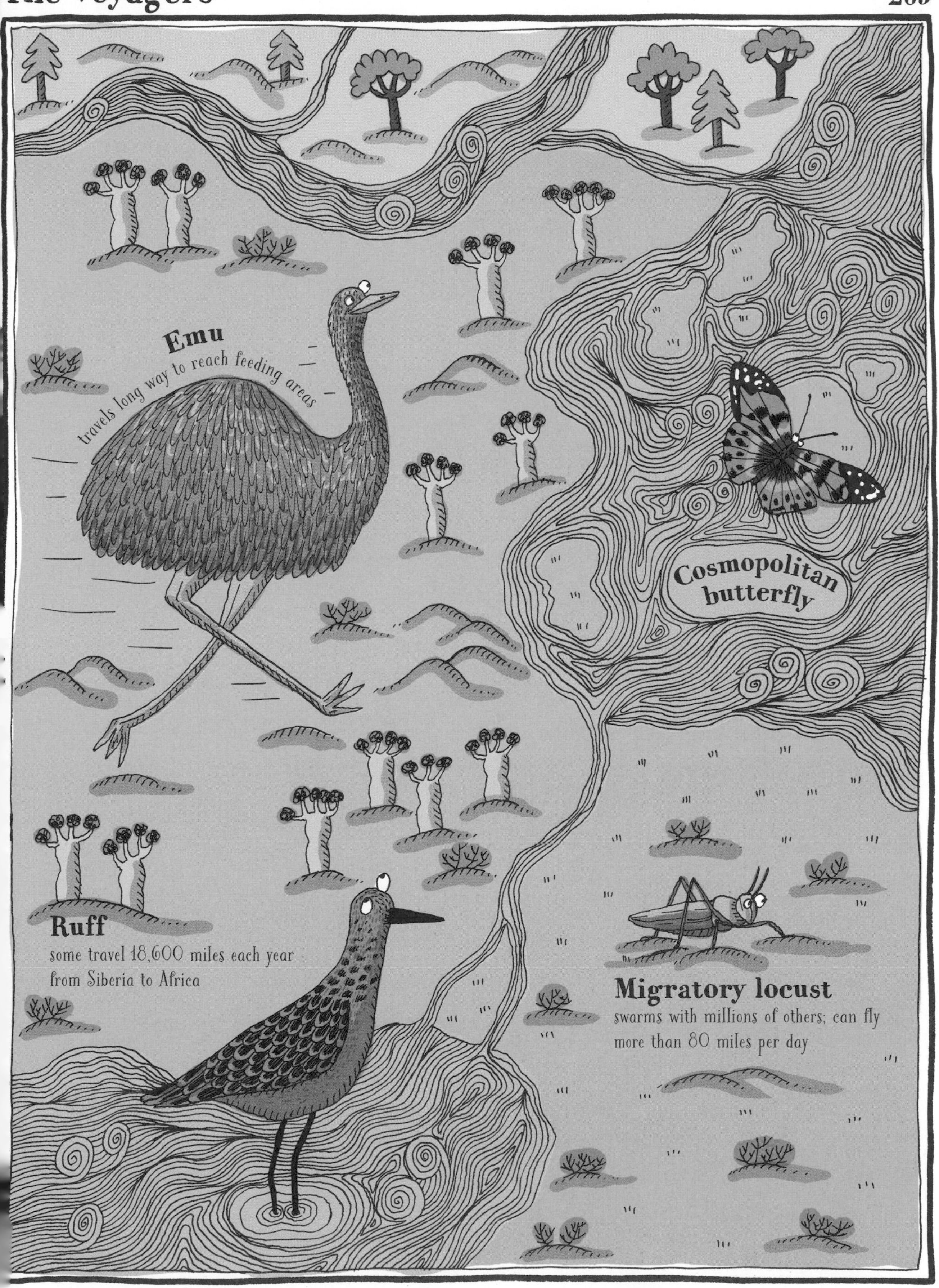
Emu
travels long way to reach feeding areas
Cosmopolitan butterfly
Ruff
some travel 18,600 miles each year from Siberia to Africa
Migratory locust
swarms with millions of others; can fly more than 80 miles per day

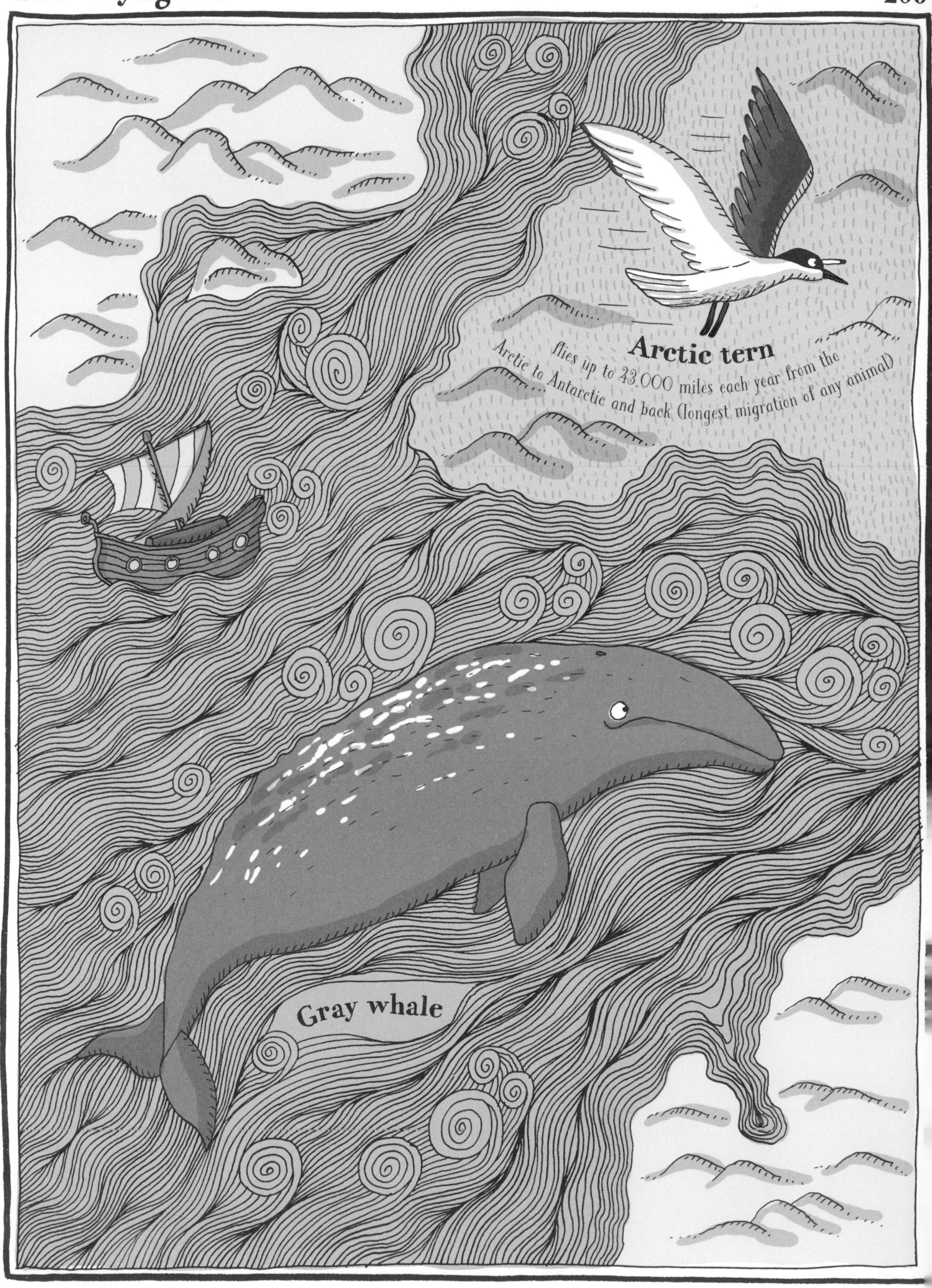
Arctic tern
flies up to 43,000 miles each year from the Arctic to Antarctic and back (longest migration of any animal)
Gray whale

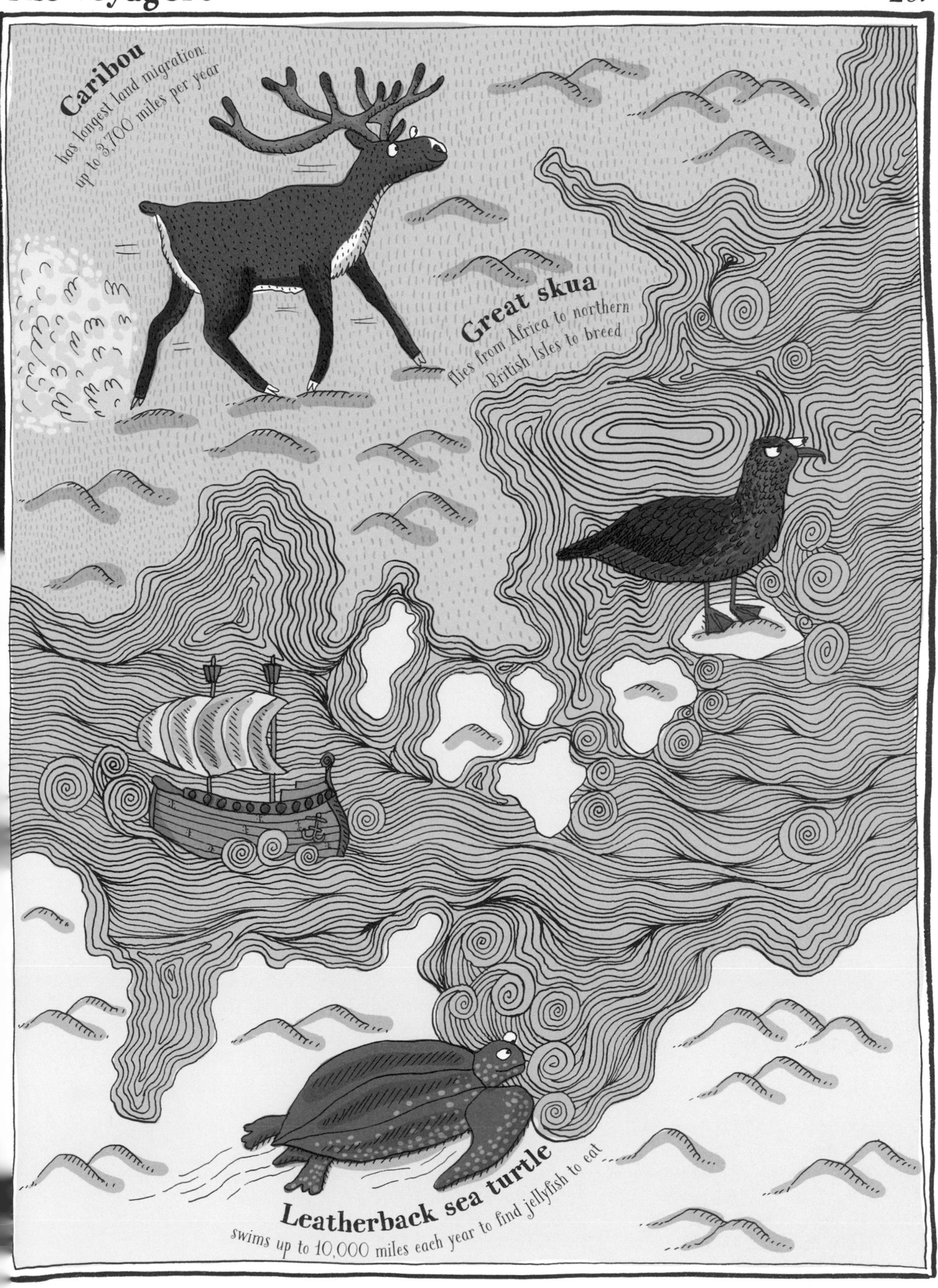
Caribou
has longest land migration:
up to 3,700 miles per year
Great skua
flies from Africa to northern
British Isles to breed
Leatherback sea turtle
swims up to 10,000 miles each year to find jellyfish to eat

Barn swallow
flies from northern to southern hemisphere to avoid winter (at speed of 200 miles a day)
Monarch butterfly
travels from Canada to Mexico for winter
White stork
flies up to 12,400 miles a year from Europe to Africa and back
Canada goose
migrates with others in V-shape to save energy
Brown trout
swims from lakes to rivers or streams to lay eggs
European eel
travels 3,100 miles to lay eggs

Acknowledgments

My heartfelt thanks:
to the jury of the City and State of Geneva's 2011 grant for book illustration,
Jean Wüest, biologist, for his valuable corrections,
Cecile Koepfli (with the help of Emily and Lucia), Mirjana and Peggy Adam Farkas,
for their help with the coloring of some families

and also:
to my favorite sister,
my mother and my father for their constructive criticism and unconditional support,
Aldo for his advice and his comforting presence,
and to all my friends for their help and encouragement, many and varied:
Alain, Bichon, Anne HB, Aurélia, Barbara, Benjamin, Cécile, Cristina, Franky,
Ignacio, Jean-Marie, Jess, Matthew, Melanie, Mirjana, Moudja, Olga, Peggy, and Valerie

—A.B.

Index

Wide Eyed Editions
www.wideeyededitions.com

Illustrated by Adrienne Barman
Designed by Pascale Rosier

First published in Switzerland in 2013 under the title *Drôle d'encyclopédie*
by Editions La Joie de Lire SA, 5 Chemin Neuf, CH-1207 Genève, Switzerland

First published in the United States by Wide Eyed Editions,
an imprint of Quarto Inc.,
276 Fifth Avenue, Suite 206, New York, NY 10001.
www.wideeyededitions.com

ISBN 978-1-84780-696-3

Illustrated digitally

Set in Didodot and Bookeyed Martin

Printed in Shenzhen, Guangdong, China

3 5 7 9 8 6 4 2